DEDICATION

To all the vulnerable women seeking openness in others, and the ones who crave raw human emotions. To Dr. Frackman, thank you for helping me bloom little by little, discovering my true self in the process.

TABLE OF CONTENTS

LETTERS I'LL NEVER SEND

AN ANTHOLOGY

Edited by
Jackie Bluu

LETTERS I'LL NEVER SEND
Copyright © 2023 by UNMASKED BOOKS

ISBN: 979-8-218-23960-2

Printed in the USA by 48 Hour Books
(www.48HrBooks.com)

Content Guidance: This anthology explores aspects of mental health, and contains depictions of alcohol, sexual assault and rape, miscarriage, death (including child death), terminal illness, and hospitalization. Please read with care.

INTRODUCTION

Greetings Friends!

First, I'd like to thank you so much for investing your time and money in *Letters I'll Never Send*. If you're here, you were perhaps drawn to the title, curious to discover what sorts of letters hid between these pages. You may be a contributor—excited to uncover what other fellow contributors privately shared or expressed, realizing in the process, that you've experienced the same sentiments as the letter's author. Or you may have just stumbled upon this anthology by chance, uncertain about what lays ahead, what secrets might be revealed, or how some of these pieces might inadvertently resonate with you. No matter how you got here, I am glad you came, and I hope that, even if you're not touched by all the pieces in this book, that you are maybe affected in some way, by at least one.

This project started as a fleeting thought, as most of my projects do, then morphed into an idea that I had to entertain deeper. I am intrigued by the simple components that make up our daily lives, like having an awkward encounter with a stranger, writing in a diary about an incredible day, or nervously awaiting a reply to a daring text. I'm also fascinated by letters (handwritten or typed) and how their modern rarity intensifies their beauty even more. And so, I thought, what if I created a project compiled of letters, in various forms? What if it included personal essays, diary entries, short poems, or even short self-reminders? I fell in love with the idea as I pondered on it, bringing it to fruition in my inquisitive mind, then quickly diving into extensive research on how to develop an anthology, from placing a call for submissions to compiling tons of entries to finally organizing each chapter into empathetic themes that we as humans know all too well. Each theme explores a human experience or touches on a life circumstance that we are familiar with, such as grief, guilt, resilience, reflection, and more.

We are here, on an inexplicable planet that we are forced to inhabit, having no choice but to cohabitate with our same species. We try tremendously to break from the pack, aiming to prove that we are one of a kind. And of course, we are, physically, mentally, emotionally, culturally, and so on. We differ in our taste buds, our opinions, backgrounds or languages. Our life experiences vary, and our perceptions hold distinctive meanings. But I believe our thoughts intersect from time to time, and we share periods of identical thoughts, reactions, or lessons, even if for a moment. We carry the ability to empathize with someone who recently lost a family member because we have likely lost someone in our lives as well. Similarly, we can appreciate and even strongly relate to someone's deeply exposed private thoughts written on paper. We feel seen. We love being seen because it makes us feel more connected. How ironic is it that in our determined efforts to express our individuality, we still yearn for acceptance, connection, togetherness, and maybe some form of intimacy? How extraordinary is it that in our ambitious quests to rise above the rest, we share similar stubborn habits that we'd rather entertain only in the privacy of our own home? How eccentric, yet comforting, to know that an episode in your life can resonate with millions of others?

This is my objective in forming this experiment: to combine intimate stories that differ in tone, style and mood. I decided to compile a small group of women-identifying or nonbinary contributors. What sorts of stories will these women share, and what, if anything, can we learn from them or from the project as a whole? What feelings will arise? What similar thoughts will you share? What perception will you also adopt? Which ideas will you consider? Which person will you relate to the most? Some of these passages are short streams of consciousness, while others recount traumatic or somber occurrences. Some pieces may affect you in a profound manner, while others may have no effect at all. You might find humor within some of these stories and notice anger or sentiments of abandonment and fear in others. I don't expect that you'll resonate with all of these—in fact, you may not relate to any of the stories told. But there is one minor request I'd like you to consider: While flipping through these pages of bare anecdotes, thorny confessions and nostalgic recollections, try not to judge the pieces for their merit, but for what emotions they conjure within you. Remember, this book is about connecting and relating—to the woman who is grieving her unborn child, to the abandoned daughter who envies her father's new "perfect" family, or to a friend who mourns a fading friendship. This book invites us to feel, along with the author, and experience what they've experienced through their susceptible words. Take a dive and reflect on what comes up for you, if anything. During the submission process, I received tons of emails expressing how cathartic writing these passages felt. Many submitters shared that they were grateful to have had the opportunity to release emotionally in this way, even if their piece ended up not being a part of the anthology. Maybe you'll relate to this feeling while absorbing some of these stories. Maybe... you'll be driven to conjure up a letter of your own.

CHAPTER 1
PERPETUAL BOND

"Souls bound together can't be forever torn apart by distance and neither by death."

—Patti Callahan Henry

Take a moment and think about the bonds you've established in your life—with your brother, your children, or your close friends. Do you believe that bond could remain solid no matter the distance or time? What is it that unites you so strongly to that person? Is it an unforgettable shared experience? Is it your mutual love for each other or a certain thing? Is it simply because you are related? Alternatively, think of someone you'd love to build a stronger bond with—your mother perhaps? A friend you've lost touch with? What impact does this person have in your life, and what drives the urge to preserve that bond?

I think of my bond with my own mother and how I not only wish it was healthier, but also more substantial. I wish we had watered each other's spirits at the times they were depleted, and I wish we continued to do so as we grew older. But sprouted from the roots of an unhappy and abusive home, our relationship cultivates slowly, fading most times, and plateauing other times, especially when we spend days or weeks with zero communication. Eventually we'll pick up where we left off: our usual five to ten-minute lukewarm check-ins, then we'll repeat the tepid cycle all over again. The distance between us, physically and emotionally, is far-reaching, but our unfortunate shared trauma binds us for an eternity. My mother and I are not close, not even a little bit—we're simply two strangers bound by DNA and trauma. But the flimsy rope that ties us helps maintain a modest enough distance between us—one that provides some satisfactory comfort that at least we're in each other's lives, even if for a moment in a season.

The following are some other personal stories of bonding, or lack thereof. As you read these short letters, think about the bonds each woman is describing. Imagine how they felt in the moment they scribbled those words. What comes up for you, if anything? Do you relate at all?

Dear Little One
Angela Cheveau

Dear Little One,

I have wanted to write this letter to you for a long time now, but I think I have always been too scared or too anxious to face starting it. How can you face a longing so deep with something as futile as mere acceptance? That seems like giving up. However, as time progressed, I have come to realize that some things are just not meant to be. That some things will forever hover on the vestiges of life, always remaining just out of sight and as delicate as gossamer wings.

I suppose a lot of the time, I was worried about what other people might think, and how it would seem like madness to them that I was writing a letter to you particularly. But now, with hindsight, I believe that it is only at rock bottom that you can fully appreciate the sky and it is only then, that you learn enough about yourself and about life to be able to express your soul without concern for what other people may, or may not, think. These are my words to you and to you alone, and I know that what I have to say will mean something to you because you, of all people, I am certain, would love me. Sometimes, if I try hard enough, I can feel you. I hold you close to my chest, feel the weight of your little head against my breast as I nestle you in my arms. I can smell the top of your head. You smell of milk and talcum powder and dreams.

I do dream of you. I dream of singing you to sleep while silvery moonlight spills through the window and caresses the soft hairs on your head. I love you as deeply as if you were sitting here beside me as my pen gently strokes the page in front of me. I know that in some way, you are here with me. You are as real as the dust motes twirling lazily in the stream of sunlight that filters through the window, or the splash of rainbow on the floor pooling around my feet. You are an energy, a light that is always with me yet always just out of sight, just out of reach, forever peeping around the next corner. Maybe if I only looked the right way at the right time? Our game of peekaboo always finds me the loser and you, remaining as distant as the stars. I miss you in a way that does not seem possible for someone or something that has never existed. I miss you in a way that makes my heart hurt.

To me, until now, you always were, and always have been, a possibility. I do not think that I ever truly believed that you were not. I am writing this letter to you because I want to tell you my story: Mummy's story. I want you to know that you were wanted, that you were loved and that I tried endlessly to bring you into existence. Maybe my purpose here on earth was not to be a mother and yet still, I feel the need to show you how to live. How I lived. I know that after me, there is nothing, that my story will be lost to time, my existence forgotten as thousands before me have been, and yet I want there to have been some point to my existence here. I have nobody to tell the vastness of my soul to. Only you. I want you to know that I lived, that I loved, with my whole heart, that I breathed for one special moment on this precious fragile beautiful bubble floating through space and time, and that I was grateful. Grateful for this heartbreaking, achingly beautiful journey that we call life.

Maybe I am shouting my story out into an empty sky, willing it to echo across the mountain tops, for the trees to whisper it to each other, and hoping it will carry on to the breath of the sweet spring wind, rustling through the long grasses of the sun-splashed wildflower meadow. Maybe this is all ego, the need to validate my existence here, to prove I had a point, a purpose? Maybe I hope to change a life? To spark a light in somebody whose light has also been dimmed, and then once lit, their light carries onto the next person and the next, until all at once, the whole world is illuminated by a river of light. I believe that we are all stories waiting to be told. Each of us holds a book within us — letters imprinted across the pages of our hearts, words coursing through our veins. We all want the universe to know that we existed, that we had a story, a point.

I ache for you.

You will always be my forever grief, a song never to be sung yet the music still seems to linger gently in the air. If I could only place my ear to the wind at the right time.

You exist in the words that I write to you. I am giving birth to you through language the way that I could not do in life. You exist in my words and the images that I leave behind of you. I am making you real. You exist for me writing these words and you exist for the person reading these words. You breathe amongst these words, giggle inside these sentences. Your tiny feet patter across this page like soft rain. I want you to know how to live, how to grasp this life with both of your chubby little dimpled hands and run with it. Let your soul burst open on the wind scattering blossoms. Life is a gift, every minute of every day. Do not waste a single moment of it.

To My Littlest Loves
Brittany Macbeth

As I write this letter, all of you vary in age: nine, six and four. Life is messy, wonderful and hard.

Charlie, you are struggling, with school, friends and personal battles. It's hard being a girl in this society — the need to fit in and the amount of energy you already put into worrying about what other people think concerns me. I know you don't think I know what it is like, but I was once a pre-teen too. The world was a much different place though. Just know that I am a great listener and a solid shoulder to cry on. Living with a parent one week on and off is exhausting and emotionally straining. You probably wonder if I "love" your siblings more because they have the whole "mom and dad, picture-perfect family scenario". I want you to know that this is not true — it is hard for all of us. We miss you when you're not here and always plan events to include you. So even though your parents aren't together, it doesn't make you any less a part of this family unit. Do you resent me? Do you resent your siblings? I hope you don't, but I understand how that would play out in your mind. Oh, and not to mention you're also living through a pandemic. You are a beautiful soul, kind and always have such a sensitive heart that cares for others. You amaze me every day with your strength.

Cecelia, you are a force. You test me every day with your pranks and your obsessive need to have everything in a particular way. Especially the way your mittens NEED to be tucked into your sweater and then into your coat. If not, there is a level ten crisis, all of which occurs before the bus comes to pick you up for school. You are only six, so life isn't particularly hard per se. Sure some minor issues arise on the playground, but you aren't hormonal enough yet to let them ruin your day. Maybe you will be the child that doesn't care about what people think and let things slide off your back a little easier? Nonetheless, your worries seem to be relatively small and your thirst for knowledge about all things science makes me happy. You are technically a middle child, but half the time you are the oldest. Is that hard for you? To have a sibling that lives somewhere else fifty percent of the time? I always wonder what goes through your mind because I know how deep you think. I am harder on you compared to the others. I'm trying to find that balance. It's not because I'm trying to be malicious but because I know your potential. You have the drive and determination to do extraordinary things. I'm not saying the other two don't. I just know your personality and qualities will bring you to places that I wish I could have taken myself. I see now where parents try to live out what they couldn't through their children. Never fret, I won't be "that" mom. I will support you in all your endeavors. You are strong, kind, brave and have the best sense of humor.

Benjamin, you are the baby. You'll always be the baby to me. I'll always worry a little bit more about you — you're sensitive and crumble easy. You're only four, so everything is the end of the world for you right now. You are a pandemic toddler and haven't had nearly enough interaction with the outside world. I'm sorry that I'm not the sensitive mom you may need. You and your sisters are teaching me how to be a little less hard each day. I'm still learning, too. I hope growing up in a world like this one doesn't harden you like it did me. Keep your soft spirit. Don't let the ugliness of the world drag you down, keep shining. You have such an infectious laugh and bright smile. I am eager for you to go to school to pave your own way, like your sisters, and to see where you make your mark. I never thought I would be a boy mom. I thought I was going to have a gang of girls. You challenge me. I've had to completely change my parenting tactics with you. You've taught me that not all kids fit into a certain parenting mold. I am so thankful that I get to raise you and watch you grow. You are bright, loving and full of life.

I hope you all know that I am trying my best to be the mother you all deserve. To make sure you all feel loved and supported. To know that I am a safe place but won't hesitate to tell you the truth. I apologize for the days when I am impatient, tired, overwhelmed and not my best self. I guess when I first became a mom, I was young and naïve, thinking that this was going to be a fun and easy journey filled with snuggles and laughter. It still is filled with snuggles and laughter but also many other things. Some days I question everything, and other days I feel like I have a decent handle. But then laundry piles up, meals need to be prepped, homework needs to be completed, extracurricular activities, and the list goes on. Some days I feel like I'm drowning in all the things but doing it for you three makes it worth all the lack of sleep. Anyway, I hope I'm doing this parenting thing right, but if not, that's okay too. It takes a lot to raise good humans. My hope for all three of you is that you are healthy, kind and follow all your dreams. Be happy. Always know that I love you to Neptune and back.

Sincerely,

Your very tired but grateful Mom

Your Birth Mother
Candace Cahill

Dear Michael,

I've always wondered if you ever read my journal. The one I gave your dad and mom when they took you home. I remember hours spent pouring my heart out onto the pages, feverish, hand cramping. I wanted to explain, in my own words, how I could do such a terrible thing—how I could give away my baby. I now know I was still trying to convince myself that what I was doing was right—that I was a "brave and selfless" woman like the agency claimed. Did I paint a wounded version of myself? Caught in a trap, cornered by poverty, abuse, and neglect? A woman—no, a girl really— willing to accept her inability to parent, having a lack of resources, lack of... everything, and surrendering to powerlessness? Or did I share how I feared turning into a monster—into a mother who belittles her child or locks them in a closet or drowns them in the bathtub? Because I felt like a monster. Sometimes, I still do.

When I asked your dad, years after your funeral, if he'd ever found the journal in your belongings, he said no. Did you ever see it? I wonder when it disappeared. I'm paranoid that your mom wouldn't let you have it—that she threw it away before you even knew how to read, fearful of any residual hold I might have, afraid she might lose you. Afraid of the truth.

So, I wonder, did you ever read it? And if you did, what were your thoughts?

I guess I will always wonder. Like I will always miss you, and always have.

Your Birth Mother

To My Unborn Baby Sister
Kayla Randolph

To My Unborn Baby Sister,

I almost collapsed in the middle of the street when I first learned about you. I can tell you that I never imagined I'd ever have a sister. At 19, I thought my days of new siblings, half or otherwise, were behind me. Yet, I sit here penning this.

I like to write. It's how I deal with a lot of things. Now our father, I've written about him quite a lot. But he and I, we have our story. If you want to hear it one day, I'll tell it. Until then, I'll let you two have your own.

All I will express is what I wish for you. I dream that you will have two parents who love you unconditionally, that you will always have them there for you. I dream that they will comfort you when you cry and that you never, ever have to doubt that you are a priority. I dream that you will always feel that they've got your back.

But, if they don't, or even if they do, I want you to know that you have me. Now, I know I've never had a sister before. I can't paint nails or do makeup. I can braid your hair though. I can show you how to bake. I can read to you. When you're older, I can read with you. I can take you shopping or out for ice cream, even if I am slightly lactose intolerant, but no biggie, right?

I can help you with your homework. I'm a good listener. I give decent relationship advice and the best Christmas presents. I know how girls can be cruel and boys can be mean. Well, everyone can be mean sometimes. I know what it's like to get your period and shave your legs for the first time. I know the best movies and shows for any occasion and appreciate the value of good snacks.

So, all of this is to say that I'll give you my best shot. All of this is to say that I can't wait to meet you.

Love,
Kayla

Dear Lost One
Taisha Ostler

Dear Lost One,

I like to think of you as a girl. A daughter to bring a bit of balance to this house now filled with boys. We longed for you then, and I still feel the weight of your loss in quiet moments. Moments when my arms feel too light, like they haven't lifted as much as they would, had I been a mother of three. It doesn't matter that I have wrapped my arms around two gangly, tall, sometimes stinky but always amazing boys for twelve years since you slipped away—you were loved before you took root in my womb, and I mourn that my belly did not swell with you the way it did with them.

Before they kicked and rolled inside of me, you were the miracle of life that fulfilled the beginnings of our seven-years long journey toward parenthood. You were only with me for eight short weeks—nestled into the folds of my uterine wall, working hard to pump blood through your newly formed ventricles, positioning your digestive system, forming your bronchial buds (that should have become lungs for screeching at birth), dividing the cells that would become your brain—near the time in development when your skin and features would start to contour into a small mixed-up version of me and your dad. We were so close to having our parenting hopes realized, when your tiny heart gave out.

My heart keeps beating, pumping me through the ups and downs of life. And I hold tightly to eternal promises of my faith that tell me that you have a spirit, and that in some other realm beyond this life, we will be resurrected and reunited. I hope it's possible. I like the idea of somehow feeling your weight in my arms, but I don't really know how it all works. I'm beginning to think that maybe my thinking of you at this moment is what eternity is all about. Or perhaps my writing about you is what makes you continue on.

Two years after we'd lost you, when I had your twin brothers, I felt like I was surrounded by angels. Were you there?

After they were born, your dad bought me a ring that I wear on the middle finger of my right hand. It has three stones: one blue and one red, that represent our baby boys, and a clear one in the center for you. Perhaps, whenever I look at that stone and think about what might have been, you live on and maybe that is enough.

Maybe that is all you were ever meant to be, a brief encounter to remind me to be present for each corporeal moment that I now get to ruffle the hair of two boys fully formed and realized in the flesh.

Of course, these ruminations do not let me mourn your loss any less, but whatever the grand plan, I am grateful for it all: the sobs that came after a numb walk to my car when

I learned that you would not become the size of a plum, or pear, or watermelon like the baby books said you would; grateful for your dad's strong arms that lifted me up when he found me sitting on the stairs crying; grateful for the way my body ached after the doctor performed a D&C to remove a portion of tissue that refused to let go. Those heartaches elevate the joys: the pure elation I felt when I heard your brothers screech at birth; the blurry peaceful nights when I nursed one boy and then the next; the laughter that often fills the once quiet corners of our household.

I will always mourn that our time together was short, but I also cherish it. Together, we are part of an ongoing story, a story that I feel lifted by and privileged to take part in. After all, when I really consider it, little lost one, for eight short weeks you and I were a part of miracle-making.

I love you,

Mom

CHAPTER TWO
FAMILY PORTRAIT

*"Like all the best families, we have our share of
eccentricities, of impetuous and wayward
youngsters and of family disagreements."*

—Queen Elizabeth II

What does your family portrait look like? How would you describe your family? Are you a close-knit bunch who find any excuse to get together and celebrate? Does your family fit somewhere in the middle—not constantly lurking around, but close enough to dump a pile of laundry or drop by for Sunday dinner? Or would you label your tribe as dysfunctional—not a tribe at all, but an estranged group of acquaintances who just happen to be genetically affiliated?

My family relationship falls in the last category—highly malfunctional and largely estranged. We do not gather for the holidays, nor do we chitchat over the phone for any amount of time. In fact, I don't believe any of us have even a slight idea what is happening in each other's lives. An arbitrary happy birthday text once in a blue moon serves as a fleeting reminder that we are still alive. We assume, it seems, that we will surely be notified, by someone, somehow, if one of us passes on. Troubling, some might think. But I have grown to accept our impaired familial fate throughout the years, slowly understanding that every family is not created equal. Some families will share tons of gut-busting laughter and banter; others will engage in silly decades-long rivalries; and some will show up for each other in times of mourning, tribulation, or anguish. I have gone on to build my own chosen family over the years, with long-time friends and newcomers who have made quite an impact in my life. These are the people who I choose to spend quality time with, visit during the holidays, and celebrate memorable occasions with. Our family portrait may vary from your typical example, but I am certainly grateful to have developed my own circle of reliable humans.

The following pieces depict some other family interactions that you might find to be awfully unique or strikingly relatable. As you read these stories, reflect on your interactions with your own inner circle. How's your family life? Have you checked on a loved one recently? What is the last thing you said? How do you think you could improve this aspect of your life? Or how can you strengthen it even more?

Stifling Rampant Wildflowers
Savannah Moix-Rogers

Baby blue and fenced in by
rickety, chain-linked barriers that stifle rampant
wildflowers beneath them. That's my home.

Mobile trailer housing my formative years,
positioned across from my father's failing
small business. To him, not small.

Family photographs portray a shared haggardness,
a result of no financial stability.

Shutters hanging loosely without a care.
Exterior holes stealing glimpses of abuse.

Dingy clothes passed between hyper-vigilant children,
tattered by time and frequent use.
An involuntary communal wardrobe of sorts.

The old Polaroids foster tearful laughs.

Vitriolic tantrums erupting between grown adults
led to feuds over which trusted

neighbor to call for back-up support.

Hiding in closets waiting for care.

It doesn't take too much effort
to forge man-made holes in walls.
I have watched it countless times.

More effort is necessary to self-soothe.
Still haven't perfected this one yet.

How Do You Want Me to Be Silent?

Sophie Jupillat Posey

Mother, you tell me to be silent, but you do not tell me how.

My mouth is shut, but there are layers of silence that speak,

As stratified fossils waiting for eons to be discovered.

My mouth is shut because you do not want to hear my pain,

Hear the inflection in my voice, hear my questioning of your dubious authority,

Mother. You do not want insolence, you say,

So, I will be silent. Would you have me silent as a grave?

Your words will bury me in a coffin of your virulent contempt.

Then my silence would give consent.

Would you have me silent as the dead?

I am weary and dead from your torture of my character,

My principles which you transform into crimes.

To you, my silence is golden, but to me, it is a hush of defiance.

You recognize it, so you pull my hair, beat your fists on my arms,

Spit in my face as you scream about insolence.

I am still silent, but my eyes cannot be mute.

I could demand my body to be silent: arms limp, head at rest,

Eyes downcast, back straight.

My silence would read as acquiescence.
I could demand my mouth to be less frowned.
I could demand my facial muscles to not be tense.
I could demand my jaw to not be clenched.
I could demand my hands to not be curled, nails digging in my palms.
Every limb could shed and don a silence,
Subtleties that will never satisfy you anyway.
So, I ask again: How do you want me to be silent,
So that you can truly love me? You have never answered me.

Sincerely, B.
Brianna Malotke

Father,

One day, down the road, I might be able to share my feelings out loud, or even just mail this letter. But for now, I find myself reeling with emotions every time I think of the things that I want to say to you. It's hard to put them into words, but I'm going to do my best.

When you took photos at your wedding, it wasn't the first time I felt alone, but it has probably been the most memorable. I saw you standing there with your new wife and her two young kids while I sat in the pews. I took in that moment. I would now be the forgotten part of your family. I felt alone, discarded. I was an adult now, there was no need to include me in your new family. I had only met her kids a couple of times, and her not that much more. I'm not sure why I was even included as a bridesmaid, I had never had a full conversation with her before. But I was happy for you, for you to finally have what I thought you wanted – a complete family.

I'm sad that you've made me feel like I was never enough. That two people, a father and a child, couldn't be a complete family. You look really happy with them; my

Facebook feed is full of the photographic evidence. Were you simply waiting for me to leave the nest? Growing up, you were a great dad. You were involved, always driving me from one activity to the next. You pushed me, staying on top of my studies, and while you felt I should pursue something else in college, you were supportive nonetheless and always showed up when I wanted you there. But then I graduated, and moved a few states away, and you suddenly had a new family.

I'm angry with how easily it seems you've replaced me. It's frustrating, having all these emotions roll through me when I think of our almost nonexistent relationship. You're my dad and I should be happy that you're not spending your life alone. But I'm still mad. I'm confused as to why I feel this way, why I'm so angry at you having this new family. I know you were too young to be a dad, and didn't expect me, but it still hurts to see you look so happy with them. I'm an adult child from a one-night stand, who's closer in age to your wife than her kids. I'm the outcast looking in. And I'm angry.

But here's the thing. While sometimes I feel alone, and discarded, I also feel sad that there's so much distance between us. Other times I start out thinking I'm upset with the situation, but I become angry with you for not being the parent and understanding my feelings without me expressing them to you. In the end, I know you'll never ask the questions that will prompt the words I've wanted to share.

So, for now I'll write this letter to you, and hide it away in a box of keepsakes. Maybe one day I'll read it to my therapist. We've already talked about some of this before, and we'll dive deeper into my feelings on the topic. Or maybe one day I'll simply send it you — I'll be brave and mail this off to you. I'm afraid of how you'll respond though. So, I'll just set this aside. For while I feel all these emotions, bravery is not one of them. I hope you understand.

Sincerely, B.

Your Daughter, Maery
Maery Rose

Dear Leif,

I received your card on my birthday and wanted to let you know how much your apology for the "errors of your youth" meant to me. I didn't expect you to apologize for your decision to put me up for adoption, but I was glad you addressed the elephant in our relationship.

However, you also said I was "fortunate to have been chosen by a fine couple who loved me." In reality, my adoptive father was an alcoholic, while my adoptive mother was depressed and distant. I grew up believing I was a space alien sent to live with an earthling family as an experiment. I prayed every night for the mothership to come get me, but when no one showed up, I went searching for my birth mother. Inadvertently, I found you.

Your youngest daughter, Susan, was assigned to accompany me to your ranch for our first meeting—probably because she'd come to Minnesota to meet me six months earlier, and I was more comfortable with her than the rest of my newly found family. When Susan and I drove up to your driveway, you were cleaning the horses' paddocks, and looked as though you'd just walked out of an old western.

You wore a cowboy hat, half chaps, and jeans that were tucked into worn cowboy boots that nearly reached your knees.

When you put your arms out to pull me into a hug, I flinched, an instinctive reaction. The men in my life haven't been kind. But your hug was warm and safe. I contrasted this with my first husband, who once threw my cat against the wall because she jumped on the bed. Later it was me he pressed against the wall, his hands around my throat.

When you pushed me back out to arm's length, you studied my face, and said, *"You sure look like your mother when she was your age."*

I had no idea what my mother had looked like back then, but I nodded and smiled.

I write all this because I want you to understand how much that first meeting meant to me. How I took in every detail of you, your home, and your life, imagining how things might have been if you hadn't left me.

Like a lot of little girls growing up during the time of Roy Rogers and Dale Evans, I ran around in vinyl cowboy boots, a black felt cowboy hat, with a holster and cap gun strapped around my waist. I loved the idea of riding the open range, the quiet solitude of it, and wanted to have a horse that came running whenever I whistled or said their name. Now I have two horses. Neither of them comes when I call.

It was easy to build a fantasy life when I had no information about who I was or where I had come from. I didn't know that the girl who made little sense in the world I lived in would have made perfect sense in yours.

As we walked around the ranch, I saw a sandy riding arena and counted six quarter horses on your property. It was a cowgirl wannabe's dream. I watched how your horses approached you. Their ears were upright and forward; they were curious and unafraid. They didn't duck their heads away or hesitate to approach. Your old gelding nudged your hat, and it fell to the ground as he then checked your pockets for treats. You rubbed behind his ears, your lips moving with soft words and clucks. I studied you and your horses and felt several bricks fall from the wall I'd built around myself.

When Susan and I returned to Tucson, I excitedly described how the day had gone to your two other daughters. They told me I was romanticizing you. *"You see a rugged cowboy. You aren't seeing HIM."* Followed by, *"You're the lucky one. I wish they'd given me up for adoption."*

It was said flippantly. My sister likely doesn't remember saying it, but I have never forgotten. I felt like I'd been bucked off a horse and was lying on the ground, frantically telling my shocked lungs to breathe.

Your daughters told me about their childhoods, the raging arguments between you and their mother. You ended up abandoning all of them too. I'd been eager to hear about their lives, but not like this.

Maybe you've changed, at least that's what I hope. Because you, father dear, helped me make sense. I'd searched for home and found it. At least, I thought I had. The desert isn't really my home. I know that now. Just as I know that the feeling of finding home, belonging, or fitting in is something that comes and goes.

People are a blend of genetics and the influence of the parents who raised them. But the choices we make in our lives also define us. You made a choice that changed the outcome of my life. I don't know whether the outcome would have been better if you and my mother had kept me. It doesn't matter. I choose to love you.

-Your daughter,

Maery

Greetings from the Therapy Office

M. A. Dubbs

Hi Mom!

I am writing from the office of my new therapist. It's been a bit chilly here, but the company is warm. Today I tried setting boundaries for the first time! It's so different than what we have at home but that's the point of this trip, right? The sights are amazing and exotic! Self-compassion, healthy-functioning, healing, peace. I'll admit I've gotten a bit homesick, though. Part of me misses the chaos and dysfunction: the white noise of my childhood.

But despite my sickness, I know I'll get used to this quiet. The fresh perspective is doing me good. It's hard to write this but I don't think I'm coming back. I'm not trying to hurt you, but I'm happy here. I really think you should visit, though! I can even help you get here. But I know you like where you are. Stuck in the heartland of Tornado Alley. Seeking safety in the storm you've always known. Well, I'm out of room but I'm thinking of you. Try to write when I can! Wish you were here!

—Your daughter

CHAPTER THREE
GROWING APART

*Seasons change, people grow together
and grow apart, life moves on.*

—Alexandra Elle

The way I see it, growing apart simply means you are growing. Better to grow than to remain stagnant, right? You may be growing older, maturing, or maybe your values have changed. You may no longer share similar views as your childhood best friend or find that you and your partner of many years are no longer compatible.

I believe that the process of growing apart can be heartbreaking—I know the feeling all too well. I've experienced my fair share of relationships that gradually came to an end, from failed intimate high-school relationships to college friendships to close family members. As a person who struggled with the effects of loss and deep emotional attachment, those "breakups" were devastating. It was difficult for me to come to terms with my new reality at the time—that a person who had been such a huge presence in my life for years will now suddenly be absent. I felt alone, discouraged, and plainly hurt. I recall finally building up the courage to end my years-long toxic relationship with my very first boyfriend and how terrified I was of losing such a critical player in my life. My future seemed terribly grim without him. I also think back to the awkward knot that twisted in my belly each time my former best friend and I ran into each other on campus, on our way to class, or at social events.

It had never felt like a painless journey. But I learned to acknowledge these bitter experiences as part of life's growing process. I am now much better equipped to handle the end of a relationship without completely falling apart, and I realize that once one door fully closes, there is always another opportunity to open a new one—exploring a promising friendship, working on a strained relationship with a family member, or gaining a new love interest.

Some of the people I've lost touch with have tiptoed back into my life, and we have grown for the better. Some, like my husband, have grown along with me over the years, weathering all the heavy storms thrown our way. Others remain neatly locked in my thoughts, with the occasional photo popping up on my phone as a reminder of the great times we shared together. I can now smile and appreciate those moments while reminiscing, rather than pout about their unfortunate outcome. All of this, I guess, is to say that when the seasonal relationships start to fade, it is okay to let them run their course. It might even end up being the best decision for both parties. And if you and that estranged person are meant to reconnect someday, then well, all is not lost after all.

Love Always, Justine
Justine Manzano

Dear W,

I can't say I saw it coming, although I should have. The signs were all there, but I wore tinted glasses of kinship, and I always thought we'd see it through. I thought the family tie we'd declared long ago could keep us fighting life at each other's side.

But then you were gone.

The last time you said anything with meaning to me, I was lying in a hospital bed. I'd just had a C-Section, my son bursting into this world with all the drama you always said I couldn't shake. You held him in your arms and told me you were proud of me.

You'd never said anything like that to me before and it meant the world to me. You were the brother of my heart, a man who wasn't committed to me by blood nor marriage, but who simply enjoyed my company. You'd been there for everything. All the big events. Everything that mattered.

The last time I laid eyes on you was also at a hospital. You abandoned an important appointment because my son had broken his arm. It was kind, but odd. At the time, we hadn't spoken about anything more important than a damn video game in nearly three years. You were around, but your presence had lost its depth — a drizzle after a pouring rain.

Even as I thanked you, I mourned your loss. You weren't my best friend anymore. I truly believed you would always be my brother. But you faded. Slowly, but with intent, you disappeared. I've heard things about your life, and even though I know you don't still live there, I look for you every time I pass your old home. And I miss you.

We may never speak again, but if this message somehow finds you, even when I no longer know how to find you, I hope it finds you well. I will always hate you for leaving me. But I will also always love you. We were always more complex than we ever wanted to admit.

Love Always,

Justine

Wading
Emily Hockaday

When I crossed the reflective threshold
you were supposed to come too. When I submerged
beneath the meniscus, you should have dived in
instead of measuring the displacement. I know
it wasn't healthy. But you should have come all
the way through and pulled me out. I'm not blaming
you, but there is a certain amount of complicity.
For years after you left, I imagined a hurt much
greater than what was really inflicted. I wanted those years
to have been worthwhile. Do you convince yourself
sometimes that you miss me, too?

Mulch for Winter Blooms
Joanell Serra

Partner, I owe you time, so we walk together on an unseasonably warm February morning. The daffodils are out, leaning into our presence as we pass, like girls waving. These walks of ours are quiet, done with the arduous tasks of raising children and putting our parents into the ground. What's left to discuss? Air purifiers, the crumbling government, dinner.

The camellias have bloomed so early, heads already dropping to the ground. I lift a flower to examine the vulvar layers still popsicle pink, though browning at the edges. Remember the two bushes, brought home years ago? It was in the first house, where the rose bushes pricked the baby's fingers. He kept trying to hold one in his tender hands.

I carried home two Azaleas in tubs, my first attempt to plant something. I mused on the botanical warnings:

Flower heads will swell in early spring
Remove dead and diseased branches
Transplant only in early spring or fall
Be careful not to damage the growth bud

I'm thinking we did everything wrong.

I've lost sight of you now, so far ahead on the path. You don't notice me on my knees collecting the fallen flowers, because I can't bear to think of them dying alone.

CHAPTER FOUR
FOND MEMORIES

Take care of all your memories.
For you cannot relive them.

—Bob Dylan

We all carry at least one warm memory that will live in our hearts forever. They vary, from silly childhood escapades to unforgettable road trips, to random snapshots of a meaningful moment in time.

Some of my fondest memories live in my childhood, growing up in Haiti. A lot of them involve my long-deceased father, and each one holds a special place in my heart. My most cherished memory, which I recount in blurry images, places us sitting across one another on the second floor of a sunset-lit restaurant. There, for the very first time, I took full delight in the most scrumptious tomato tuna melt ever. Growing up, I was accustomed to only eating home-cooked meals: *du riz blanc à sauce pois noir*[1], *du riz djon djon avec lambi*[2], *macaroni au gratin, legumes avec maïs moulin*[3], and

---

[1] White rice with black bean stew
[2] Mushroom rice with conch
[3] Cornmeal with legumes (cabbage, carrots, peppers, etc.)

plantain porridge, are among some of the delectable delicacies that I often enjoyed. So, eating out, let alone a tuna sandwich, was a rare and unfamiliar experience in my household. That warm afternoon, I remember the sunlight hitting me and my father in just the right spots, warming our faces as we chatted about father-daughter things that I wish I could recall. I remember him enjoying the look of joy and enthusiasm on my face as I savored each bite of my sandwich. I remember it was the first and last tuna sandwich that I indulged in for many years.

I have a slight obsession with tuna sandwiches now—my cabinet is always chock full of cans of tuna, and my husband and I probably eat tuna sandwiches at least once a week. I doubt I'll ever grow tired of eating them. And perhaps, in a strange, peculiar way, this is how I keep my father close and alive—by indulging in delicious tuna sandwiches every so often. Perhaps this is my subconscious way of keeping that memory of us alive.

What's your fondest memory? What stands out the most? The following two pieces are short, sweet, yet impactful, holding so much depth in memories. Sometimes, the smallest and most transient moments are the moments that one remembers forever. Take this into account as you pore over the authors' most indelible reminiscence.

Postcard from Zurich
Robbin Farr

I am returning to Paris
to attend to the estate
of our friend Johannes
and traveling through Zurich
where years ago
we held over on our way
to holiday in France.

I recall how shuttered houses
rose from the mountainside
bright as the fields
of Alpine snowbells
as we descended
into early morning
Flughafen Zurich.
It was my first trip abroad.

You savored your role
as tour guide
and days later, we abandoned all
to love beneath the striped awning

of Café Marie on Rue Gabrielle,
all of Paris as witness.

I wonder will I post this note
and chance it will reach you
in St. George? Do you think
fondly of Zurich as I do?

Do you remember
having laugenbrezel
for our breakfast?

It's Been 66 Years
Abigail Hagler

Dear Chris,

You were the first handsome boy I ever saw - or were those just adolescent hormones kicking in? I also noticed Peter, but I saw his obituary in *The New York Times* about a year ago . . .

Anyway, here's what I wanted to let you know. On the first day of school, Joaquin tried to beat me up and you protected me. Joaquin got kicked out, I was unhurt, and I have been in love with you ever since.

It's been 66 years - do you remember saving me?

Abby

CHAPTER FIVE
GRIEF-STRICKEN

*"We bereaved are not alone. We belong to the
largest company in the world – the company of
those who have known suffering."*

—Helen Keller

Grief and I need no introduction. We have been
acquainted long before I even understood its meaning and
effect. Grief tackled me at a most vulnerable age, at a time
when an eighteen-year-old's primary concern should be the
bright future that lays ahead, not coping with the sudden
absence of their sibling.

My father passed away when I was seven years old. I
don't recall much of the day I learned the news other than
my godmother walking gracefully toward me as she arrived
home from work, placing me on her lap, and gently
expressing to me that my Papi had gone to heaven. I don't
think I processed her words or the situation at that time. And
I honestly don't believe I ever did—not until the extremely
untimely death of my little brother, Sebastian. Nothing about
his death made sense, and I was left reeling, begging for
explanations, any explanation: about his cause of death,

about the meaning of life and death, about my own and other loved ones' expiration dates. Obsession was an understatement. My mental health derailed after years of buried pain, and eventually, grief won. At least for a noticeable amount of time.

I think I hit rock bottom when I ended up in the New York Presbyterian behavioral psych unit for a few weeks. Grief alone didn't land me in the ward of course—there were other life circumstances that played an important part, plus past trauma and varied unfortunate events. But grief was the catalyst—the driving force of my entire psychological warfare.

Grief is vicious. And unfortunately, we're due to experience it one way or another. Years of therapy and continuous self-work has helped me cope with the lingering effects of my little brother's death. Every now and then, I relapse, and am crippled by frightening visions of another loved one resting lifelessly in an open casket. I stand paralyzed in fear for a few minutes. But I'm training myself to not live in that unpleasant space for too long. I'm learning that, trauma from grief may not be completely inescapable, but it is manageable. I'm discovering that grief is a process—an inevitable path that one must travel through and learn to navigate with mindful awareness and humble acceptance. I continue to grapple with that last part though. Learning to accept any, including my own imminent death, comes with daily reminders to just take advantage of every single moment. I believe that is grief's medicine: taking in each moment, experiencing every single feeling, living for those who cannot. There will come occasional bumps and moments of pain, but you'll become better at managing those grief-stricken episodes over time. Grief is, after all, a process.

Are you grieving anyone in particular? What does your process look like? How do you think you'll relate to the following stories?

Letters to Sam
Kimberley Petrie

April 2021

Dear Sam,

I knew something wasn't right when I noticed you hadn't been on Twitter for three months. I thought it was odd when you didn't respond about our divorce being finalized, but I figured you'd get in touch eventually. You always did turn up, like the proverbial bad penny.

I joked with friends about how silent you'd been. You lived your whole life through social media, using it to create an alternative reality, so it really did seem quite bizarre. For weeks, I dismissed any negative thoughts by saying *"he's probably been drunk and lost his phone or doesn't haven't internet. Or maybe he really has moved away."*

In April, I started to ask around to determine when people had last spoken to you:

Me: January 26th, 2021

Your friend, Paul: Some time in February 2021

Your sister, Kirsty: Some time in February 2021

Your last tweet was on February 8th of 2021.

Paul said it wasn't unusual for friends to go a while without speaking. *"Life just gets in the way."* I also knew when Kirsty said that *"siblings don't always keep in close contact"* that you didn't make it easy for people to stay close to you.

On Thursday April 29th, I asked Kirsty to call the police and speak to someone about your lack of contact with people. I told her it was better that it came from her — she was your sister, a blood relative. I think partly that's true, but I also know that I wanted to try and keep my distance.

Things moved so swiftly from that initial call. The police called me to ascertain your state of mind. What could I say? We had been separated for five years. All I could tell them was that you are bit of a fantasist, in a world of your own, a real-life Walter Mitty. If Twitter was to be believed, you'd been headhunted for a job in New York, you were moving to Australia and had also been in hospital suffering from a broken spine.

The PC asked if you had any drug or alcohol related issues. My mind went back to when I had thrown you out and I found your gym bag in the cupboard. It was stuffed full of empty gin bottles. How could I have been so blind to it all?

"I think he was an alcoholic" I mumbled.

At 6pm I had an update. The police had visited your last known address, a flat in Torry on the south side of the city but there was no sign of anyone living there.

Had you really been in Aberdeen all this time? How could I not have seen you or bumped into you over the past few years? Surely our paths would have crossed at some point.

The phone rang again at 11pm.

The police had entered the flat and a body had been found.

■■■

Dear Sam,

The official line from the police was "a body has been found in the flat and we believe it to be Sam".

The Specialist Crime Division said they want to "officially" identify you from dental records as they don't want to put any of us through actually seeing you due to the length of time you've been there.

Going by the timeline of when people last spoke to you, it would appear that you may have been lying dead in the flat for months.

Things ended so badly between us that to my shame, I've often wondered how I would feel if you were no longer alive. I remember when I first threw you out and you bombarded me with texts and calls about how you were going to kill yourself. Every text or email would be signed *"You'll never have to hear from me again"*, *"You look after yourself"* or *"Goodbye, S"*.

I would be sick with worry, but you always turned up, infuriatingly acting as if you didn't have a care in the world. After a few weeks, the suicidal threats were just empty words and I dismissed them as soon as they came in.

The police said that there was *"evidence of alcohol at the scene"*. What exactly does that mean though? Was the flat littered with bottles? Did you die of alcohol poisoning? Or did you choke on your own vomit? Or was it something to do with your liver, cirrhosis perhaps?

I have visions of a living room littered with empty bottles, the stale smell of gin with the sickly scent of flavored tonic water, sticky carpets and the odd empty beer can on a bookshelf.

It's hard to believe that you could have been in a filthy flat when you were so particular and obsessive about things being clean when we were together. I think about how terrified I used to be about not doing the housework up to your impeccable standards.

Just like that, I'm jolted back to the place I've tried so hard to move on from. Memories of how I was treated and how nervous I felt flood back in.

After all this time, after all the hurt, I didn't realize I still had tears left for you.

And yet here I am, breaking my heart.

■■■

Dear Sam,

Today I made the mistake of googling *"body decomposition after death"*.

24-72 hours after death – internal organs decompose

3-5 days after death – body starts to bloat and blood containing foam leaks from the mouth and nose

8-10 days after death – body turns from green to red as the blood decomposes and the organs in the abdomen accumulate gas

Several weeks after death – nails and teeth fall out

One month after death – body starts to liquefy

Now all I have is a grotesque image of you in my mind. Bloated, discolored, skin blotchy, your body frail and skeletal.

How could nobody have missed you for three months? The fact that it was me, your ex-wife, who raised the alarm, speaks volumes about how you alienated yourself.

I never expected to feel like this. I'm suffocating from the weight of my emotions. My eyes constantly fill with tears; my head aches; my throat feels like it's closing. I can't breathe.

At the same time, I feel like my body is betraying me. How can I be this sad and upset about someone who hurt me so much? Do I even have a right to be upset? Is it hypocritical of me? I mean, I'm hardly the grieving widow, and yet I do feel an immense sense of... In fact, I don't know how I feel, it's like an ache, an emptiness in my chest, a feeling of being hollow.

Is this loss?

Your dad has asked if I can provide some music and stories for the funeral. Don't get me wrong Sam, there were good times. I wouldn't have married you otherwise. It's just that for every happy memory I have, I also have the harsh reality of a relationship built on anger, fear, ridicule and the threat of violence.

Those are not the types of things people want to hear at a funeral though.

In death, sinners become saints, flaws are forgiven.

So, with that in mind, I will do my very best.

Missing Beth Who Was Always Here
Paula Brown

Oh Beth,

I remember the gray-brown hair that dangled past your smiling face—no make-up or pretense required. You wore that earth mom look so well. You always said, *"I'm old as dirt,"* and you didn't mean just this lifetime. You claimed you'd been in and out of this planet since the early days, chowing down on carbon atoms with the prokaryotes. Beth, you knew all the ins and outs of most things earthly and not so earthly, healing our maladies with your hands, spinning my murky, waning chakras 'til they hummed like finely tuned watches. You had goodness running deep inside the way that water courses underground in veins beneath hard layers of rock. And humor, too, and so of course I loved you. I hung around you and your earthly and sometimes not so earthly friends, until one day you and Rob moved to the high plateau of Colorado. You settled in for the long haul beneath a couple of fourteeners — a cat on the couch and, I imagine, peace flags flying under the eaves.

I almost lost track of you then, except there were those holiday cards, and the report one year that some non-prokaryotic terrorist cell had taken up residence in your colon. Then came a stream of emails stringing over months and years, recounting endless trips crisscrossing those mountaintops, hunting for the cure for that guerrilla cell and all its tribe. And I know those light-filled hands of yours ached to heal you, but they could not. I tried to heal you from afar the way I'd learned, but I could not. The doctors with their drug cocktails and x-rays sought to heal you too, but they could not. When the terrorist cells kept popping up in some other unwanted place, and it became too much for your fast dwindling frame to read emails, you asked for silly greeting cards to hold between your sallow hands. Beth, you cashed in all your chips on laughter to bring you through. But all the funny cards I found were birthday cards, and so that year I wished you happy birthday at least half a dozen times while you laughed and breathed through all those months, until you birthed yourself into another place.

When summer came and you weren't there, I gathered two-inch brown clay pots. I painted them with blues and reds and yellows like peace flags, etched cats and suns and stars on them, and filled them up with rich black dirt. I blew carbon atoms into them with my warm exhaling breath, waved blessings over them with my eager hands, and placed them on my windowsill where the sun slid past them every day. *Did I really do those things?* Listen, I was only trying to make you laugh.

Hey Beth, I'm still here.
P.

Dear Justin
Sarena Tien

Dear Justin,

I hate that I've learned to live without you. It's been five years since you left me behind, a seedling struggling to grow when there's no sun left to stretch toward. You took your light with you, and I got lost in the shadows because grief wrapped its fingers around my roots and never let go.

Five years ago, I died in the Musée Tomi Ungerer, leaving behind a skeleton of a sister, tendrils of her broken heart still growing into the pristine white museum floor. At first, I cried at every reminder of you. Drawings on the ceiling of a Lyonnais bookstore. A Teresa Teng song in a Parisian restaurant. An art installation in a Dublin Museum. You were gone, but you still found a way to remind me of your love, even if all the memories of you split my world even farther apart. From having a sibling. To now being an only child.

I didn't even tell you goodbye before I left to teach for a year in France because I thought I'd get to see you again. I was such a damn fool. Instead, I had to tell you goodbye a thousand times a day and hope that my words would reach you. Did you see any of the messages that I left for you across Europe? The one-euro candles that I set aflame in French cathedrals and Irish churches, hoping that maybe, when the wish-worn wicks whispered, they would breathe you back to life? The note that I tucked into an origami boat and set adrift in a lake in Lyon, wondering if the makeshift funeral would make the real one hurt any less? The epitaph that I scrawled in yellow chalk in a café in Amsterdam?

If you didn't get any of my notes, I want you to know that I carry you with me, engraved in the ring on my finger, enclosed in the urn necklace around my neck, and written on my arm in second-grader handwriting, in orange marker that has long since washed away.

I wish people could see my grief. I no longer freeze, a deer in the headlights, when someone asks me whether I have any siblings. I hate that my voice is now steady when I respond, *"I had a brother, but he passed away."* I know it's been five years, but it still hurts to have to say it, because no one knows what you mean to me. How do I explain to them that you taught me how to ride a bike and how to drive a car? That you edited my essays and secretly ate all the meat from my bowl when our parents disapproved of me trying to become vegetarian? That losing you was the worst moment of my life, and that all I want is to be a sister again.

I've stopped crying at every reminder of you, but that doesn't mean that I miss you any less. Sometimes I dream of you but dreams only compound the grief. They're a fantasy that trick me into thinking you're still alive, and when I wake, I want to trade reality for a world that ceased to exist years ago. You're alive only in my memories and my imagination now, and I'm trying so hard to make sense of this sunless sky where life somehow moves on without you.

Even though you're no longer an email or a text away, I'll always remember you. I hope that you're happy now, wherever you are, and that I can be your annoying little sister again someday.

Love,

Sarena

Dear Oma
Gaby Ingram

Dear Oma,

Remember how you taught me to crochet, stitch or hook a rug while we watched TV, until the Sunday sermon announced a new day, and we'd giggle ourselves to sleep?

What fun we had! You showed me that it was okay to sip coffee through a sugar cube, to eat jam without bread, to lick icing off a cake. That it made perfect sense to return from a trip abroad with 20 pounds of sugar in your suitcase. Indeed, food was the answer to everything: chocolate eased menstrual cramps; sugar calmed nerves; butter held body and soul together. You firmly believed that bacon was the basis of a healthy diet, and that anything that cropped up despite a bacon-laced diet could be addressed with a Melissengeist.

Your wisdom stretched far and wide, loaded with information, like how potatoes were to blame for dogs dying of distemper; that wet hair would give me pneumonia; that Russians ate babies; and that reading too many books led to insanity.

Your version of war was one of great adventure. Your take on men was that they were ridiculous but necessary.

You taught me that your youngest daughter was fragile and needed my help; that everything could be tolerated if you turned it into a joke; that no one, Russians excluded, did hurtful things intentionally. You also taught me that there were a million factors which made people the way they were, a gazillion reasons for why people did cruel or bizarre things. There was nothing one could do, except learn to dodge the bullets. You always advised that one should remain true to one's roots, but it didn't hurt to emulate the upper class, to bring a bit of style into one's life. You never left the house without a hat to indicate that you were a lady.

You were living proof that a woman traveling the world by herself could have a jolly good time. Your missives from overseas taught me to read a script that was no longer used, to decipher sentences without punctuation. You never worried about the intricacies of grammar, never mentioned the importance of education, and maintained that a woman could have a career which did not involve taking care of people.

You forgot to explain though, that sometimes life would need to be taken seriously. That not all subjects were appropriate for joking. That a marriage could be based on love, passion and understanding. That there were shortages more devastating than a lack of food. That, a gazillion reasons notwithstanding, people bore responsibility for their behavior. That the wounds of fear and deprivation left scars that ran deep beneath the veneer of a good natured bon vivant — scars that the officiating doctor never suspected when he listed "adiposity" under "cause of death".

And you neglected to tell me who I could turn to when you were gone, or what I should do when neither the bacon nor the Melissengeist brought adequate results.

P.S. I Still Love You
Brianna Little

Dear Sister,

My better angels urge me to give you grace. You were young, only one week out of high school, and having fun with your friends at the lake. I try to think about how alive you must have felt brimming with potential and plans. You weren't much of a planner though. You lived life fully in the moment. I wonder if in one of those moments you had lost your contacts in the water, because the coroner made no mention of them in his report. I bet you thought you could handle driving home without them because you knew the way, and teenagers have that sense of unearned confidence. You especially. When you stopped at the stop sign with your friend in the passenger seat beside you, did you complain about the late afternoon sun in your eyes? Did you see the Suburban coming towards your Corolla at the last second when you pulled out to cross the highway? I no longer believe in a god, but still, I pray that you didn't. I pray tearfully that you died instantly and blissfully unaware that your car rolled across four lanes before landing in a ditch.

What were you thinking? Can't you see what you've done to us? To say *"it's all fun and games until someone gets hurt"* sounds so glib and cliché. And, yet here we all are. You had your fun and games and the rest of us got hurt. To speak ill of the dead is in bad taste, but I cannot escape the bitter taste on my tongue that comes when I think of you. I cannot escape the anger and the helplessness that I buried for 24 years since you made that choice.

You destroyed our parents. Instead of cheers of joy while reading college acceptance letters, I remember how our mother screamed. Tears streamed down her face, and she clawed at our dad and ripped his shirt. *"Fix it, David!"* She demanded desperately. *"Fix it! My baby is dead! Fix it!"* Because dad can fix anything, you know. He's smart and clever. But he couldn't fix this, and he never recovered. I want you to know that mom didn't get out of bed for three months. She didn't go back to work for a year. Dad had to go back to work, but I don't know how he did it. All I know is he came home after work every day and disappeared into the bedroom to be with mom.

You shattered my childhood. I was only seven years old, but I knew what death meant. Grandpa died the year before, remember? But worse than losing you, I lost mom and dad, too. My clearest memory of the aftermath of your death was their bedroom door closed. They got to grieve together, and they were so devastated by your loss that I was cut adrift. I had to figure out food for myself; I had to pack my lunch for school; I had to take care of myself. Our parents didn't acknowledge my existence for a few years. I didn't have the luxury of being a child because your carelessness robbed me of it. I never got that back.

I want you to know that your passenger suffered for hours before she died, and you broke her family, too. I want you to know that mom never treated me the same. She holds me up to a vision of you that isn't real, so I lose every single time. I must compete with a corpse for her love and attention. I will never be as confident, beautiful, and skinny as an Angel in Heaven. I want you to know that dad locked away his emotions and only lets them out when he's drunk, and I'm left questioning his sincerity. Silly me, though. I take what affection I can get out of him even though it hurts later. I want you to know that your stupidity left me with severe memory loss, depression, anxiety, attachment and rejection disorders, and complex PTSD. Every relationship, every conversation, every awkward silence I experience is run through the lens of pain with which you left me. A farewell gift from you to me.

You didn't choose this, but didn't you though? You could have let someone else drive you home because you weren't licensed to drive without your contacts. You could have brought your glasses as a backup. You got off easy and I resent that deeply. This was your mistake but the rest of us paid for it. Had you just taken a single moment to think ahead, you would have changed the trajectory of all our lives. You lived so in the moment that you never thought ahead, and now you live only in the fractured memories of the past.

I'm 32 years old now. You should know I'm happily married. I have dogs and chickens, some of the best friends I could ask for, and a pretty cool job. They get me through the days that you continue to make difficult. I want to forgive you, but I can't yet. There's still a child within me holding a grudge against you for taking everything from her.

I hope your lake party was worth all the pain you've caused. I bet it was fun.

Signed,

Your little sister

P.S. I still love you.

Wish You Were Here
Shelley Logan

Dear Grandma,

We're on vacation up north and we wish you were here!

I love the cool northern air on my face and the smell of
the pines. I wish I could capture a sample in a jar so I could
take it home and keep it with me always.

We went to visit your family's old cottage and saw your
second cousin once removed (or however that works). The
cabin looks different now, but your dad's old pipe is still
cemented in the hearth of the fireplace, just like you told us
it would be.

I walked down to the beach—the water is low this year,
so the beach is huge and it's a great year to look for rocks. I
scoured the coastline for Petoskey stones, and I actually
found one! Why isn't one ever enough? I couldn't stop
searching, even with one in hand. I wonder how many times
you walked this same stretch of beach before I was even
born.

The sand was cold on my bare feet, and I squealed as the
first wave reached my toes. I always forget how cold Lake
Huron is, even in August. We worked up the courage to go

swimming one afternoon, and we made it all the way out to the sand bar! I thought of how you used to say that you tried to get in the lake at least once each day, no matter how cold it was, so I knew you would be proud.

I took a walk on the trail in the woods where the Hello Tree used to be, before they widened the road and cut it down. I thought of you and Grandpa as teenagers, in your first lover's quarrel, how you went for a walk toward the sand dunes to clear your head and, on your way back, Grandpa jumped out from behind that tree and said "hello." It scared you half to death, but you weren't angry anymore; you two made up and the rest is history.

We didn't pick blueberries this year, but if we had, we would have gone to the same spot near the old airstrip. I probably would have eaten more than I put in my bucket, just like I did when I was six.

I wish we could have climbed the sand dunes and half-run, half-tumbled down, only to turn around and do it all again and again. The sand dunes are now a gated neighborhood, though, full of McMansions with paved driveways and jet skis.

I went to visit the spot on the beach, high up on the hill, just in front of the huge pine tree, where we buried some of your ashes and made a cross out of rocks. I always liked to sit there on the fallen log-turned-bench and watch the lake with you. Aunt Nancy warned me that it was gone but I just couldn't believe it. Apparently, the water was so high a couple of years ago that there was no beach at all, and she was right. I was so disappointed to see that your memorial had been washed away, but I know you're still there in spirit.

One day when I die, hopefully not anytime soon, I want my ashes buried on Evergreen Beach, too, so my kids and grandkids, and maybe even their children, will keep coming back to visit and watch the waves with us long after we're gone.

Wish you were here.

I Never Thought It Would Be Like This
Catherine Kenwell

Dear Dad,

I know you said you never thought it would be like this. Me neither.

Not sure what I expected—maybe I thought that you were going to go quickly and peacefully, like Mom did—but you're right, this has been long and excruciating. Don't get me wrong: yes, it's gone on too long and it has been horrible for all of us, but please don't ever think that you were a nuisance or a burden. It's been tough on us—your kids— because you deserve better. You deserve to leave this earth the way you lived on it, poking fun and telling jokes and sharing your wisdom, being surrounded by those who love you. It pains us to see you so frail (although I'll never say that within earshot of you; it would break your heart, I know you well enough to appreciate that).

Because of COVID, we can't visit you as a family. Hospital rules dictate one person at a time, once daily, for one hour. Everyone wants their turn. See? You're hardly a burden when there's a line-up to get in to see you. But that's it. I will not tell you how we grieve during those other 23 hours, how we wake up worrying about you, how we cry ourselves to fitful sleep.

Your heart and your lungs are failing. The rest of your organs aren't working the way they should. You can't walk. You're hooked up to oxygen and IV medication. You've told us you're not in pain, but we see you—you're fading away. Daddo, you are dying. You know that.

I wish it would happen quicker. I'm sorry—that makes me sound like a terrible daughter, doesn't it? I hope that one of these times when you doze off, you'll drift off to eternity. Maybe that wouldn't be so bad. You've even told me you'd rather not wake up.

I get it. You're the guy who played baseball until you were 83, and hockey until your late 70s. You were a natural gifted athlete and a magnificent role model. You coached countless hockey players who went on to glory. And now, your legs don't work. You're right. That seems particularly cruel.

For a guy who always had a hearty appetite, you've become picky. You won't eat. So, we've started bringing you chocolate bars, crispy squares, and pumpkin pie. All the treats you love. A couple of bites here and there, whenever you can. In our family, food is love. And boy, do we love you.

Yesterday—and you didn't know this—I brought two small hot cocoas for us to have together. You were somehow always surprised and overjoyed when I'd show up at your apartment with a couple of cups of cocoa, and I would always drink mine quickly while you managed to savor each sip. It was always our special daddy-daughter treat.

I left the two untouched cups of cocoa on your hospital tray. I had to force myself to avoid looking at them during my visit, because I knew the tears would start and I'd be sobbing uncontrollably. Instead, I just held your hand and smiled at you. Could you feel that little peck I gave you before I left? I brushed your hair back and kissed your forehead. Your hair is like Mom's now, white as snow.

I guess I'm writing this letter because I honestly don't know what else to do. I can't save you. I don't think I'm supposed to. We're at the point where anything the doctors are suggesting—the procedures, the 'fixes'—aren't going to do much to help things. They might make you more comfortable, but they're not meant to prolong your life. And I don't think you want that anyway, do you?

I don't even know how to finish this, because for once in my life I'm at a loss for words. Words don't apply here. I have my phone here beside me. I'm not sure what I'll say when the phone rings, because it will. I know. It's not long now, in the scheme of things. But it's taking forever. And you're right, I never thought it would be like this.

My Darling Mummy
Iris Leona Marie Cross

You were always an early riser. From the moment sunlight seeped through your semi-opaque curtained window, I could hear you pottering around the bedroom doing this and that. *"Why don't you stay in bed a little longer?"* I often asked. *"You're no longer a working woman."* But you found it difficult to shake off the habit of rising with the sun, even though your employment days had long since gone.

That's why I found it strange when, at almost ten-thirty that morning, I discerned no movement coming from your room. Still furious from the night before, I never inquired, choosing instead to relax in bed while listening to my favorite Sunday morning radio program "Sunday Callaloo."

Half an hour later, nonchalance turned to concern. You hadn't emerged from behind the closed bedroom door. Certain you were again being difficult, I flung open your bedroom door shouting: *"So mummy, you're not getting up...?"* Your body was slumped across the edge of the bed in a kneeling position; your face buried in the rumpled sheet, arms outstretched, palms down. Save for the ticking analog clock on the dressing table, not a murmur was detected, or a twitching muscle observed to erase the unthinkable going through my mind.

"Mummy, Mummy!" I screamed as I inched closer and closer. I touched your body; it was cold. I examined your extremities; they were blue. Kneeling beside you, I wrapped my arms around you as I often did, giving you the tightest of hugs. You didn't respond. Your body showed no signs of life because life had already expired. I rested my head on your hunched back and wept.

"Why didn't you call me? Why?" Tears streamed down my cheeks, dripping drop by drop onto the creased bed sheet. Your unmistakable scent pervaded the air. Grief and guilt consumed me. I was inconsolable.

I usually gave you your last tablet late at night when you were already in bed. Afterward, I'd kiss your forehead, tell you I love you, and tuck you under the covers while reciting the popular bedtime rhyme: "Sleep tight, don't let the bedbugs bite." You'd smile and thank me as I reached to switch off the bedroom light. I'd respond by saying you were reaping the rewards of a devoted mother. The endearing nightly exchange between us was a testament to the depth of the mother-daughter bond we shared. I had no idea that fateful night would be different from previous nights.

"Mummy, wake up. Here's your last tablet."

You opened your glassy eyes, scowled, and said: *"I took it already."*

"No, you haven't."

88

"I took it already," you insisted, raising your voice in a belligerent manner.

"No, you haven't. Look, it's in the pill organizer."

You remained adamant you had taken your daily quota of tablets. I continued to stress, without success, that you hadn't. Holding the tablet firmly between my thumb and forefinger, I reached for your mouth. Despite much coaxing, your lips remained pursed. Your obstinacy tested my patience.

"Do you think I'm trying to poison you?" I yelled, penetrating the silence of the midnight hour. By this time, I had lost both my patience and my temper. Reluctantly, you relented, but not before glaring at me and talking under your breath.

"Mummy, mark my words. From tomorrow you're on your own. I will not tolerate this nonsense again," I said, wagging my forefinger in your face.

You stared at me in defiance, so I warned you again, in staccato style. My wagging forefinger kept the beat like a metronome. *"From to- mor- row -you- are- on- your- own!"* Overcome with frustration and unprecedented rage, I stormed out of your bedroom, slamming the door with all my might. That night, I tested the strength of the door hinges.

So many times, you begged me to lie with you because you thought you were dying, and I did. Yet death met you all alone. If only our last conversation was our usual loving interaction.

I am still racked with guilt. Not knowing what happened behind the slammed bedroom door haunts me up to today. All I know is my prophetic words of warning came to pass. The next day, you were indeed on your own.

The bereavement counselor suggested I write to you for closure. Twenty-three years later, this is it. The one thing I regret is that you're not physically present to acknowledge the outpouring of my contrite heart.

Your ever-loving daughter,

Iris

CHAPTER SIX
LOOKING FORWARD

*"I know for sure that everything will
work out. No matter how crazy or bleak
the situation is, it will work out.
Everything passes, good and bad."*

—Xosha Roquemore

"It will all work out for the best." I've heard this quote countless times growing up, and it always carried the same clichéd unimportance in my mind, until I grew older and experienced firsthand a list of situations eventually working out for the best. This included unhealthy breakups, faded friendships that no longer served me, and job losses that led to much better, more fruitful opportunities. I think most of us have been there, breathing a sigh of relief for what we originally felt would be our ultimate demise, but contrarily birthed a new sense of freedom. How resilient and fascinating it can feel when an unfortunate event morphs into something beautiful? Almost like the universe is performing its own magic, doing its bidding, working in our favor in the end.

I've breathed multiple sighs of relief: when I finally realized that the long overdue end of a toxic relationship with someone close brought peace of mind rather than sadness; when I faced my fear of the unknown and moved on to a new job, discovering that it offered more rewarding advantages; or when I eventually released all the pent-up anger living within, exploring a whole new, gratifying way of existing.

Some of the following pieces are like my own experiences. Others share how their lives have improved in different ways. I wonder what will come to your mind as you reflect on those letters. How are you currently better off? Any unpleasant event or scenario that you experienced which stung for a time but then somehow improved your life, even in the smallest way?

Your (Hopefully) Ex
Rachel Friedman

Hi,

It's too late for us. I knew that months ago, but I think that you are hanging onto hope. I have nothing against such a positive emotion — in fact, I'm rather touched that you still want to be with me. The problem is that it's stopped both of us from recovering. It's odd, I suppose, to think that we can only heal by letting go of every last link to each other.

If you want to know if I loved you, I suppose that I did. I understand that this isn't a very satisfactory answer, but then I'm having trouble remembering that you used to make me happy. Nowadays, all that you seem to do is scare me. I understand that you don't mean to, but as I once said, once I'm terrified of someone, it's over. I don't know where the person that I cared about has gone. You don't seem to respect any of my boundaries anymore and learning that you're secretly smoking marijuana has made me super uncomfortable. Also, if a girl says no to something that involves her own body, that should be the end of it. I know that you think that arguing is okay in every situation, but it isn't. Sometimes it just makes the other person feel scared and vulnerable.

And that's it, I suppose. Just please promise me that you'll go to rehab and therapy before you ask anyone else out.

Your (hopefully) ex.

You Could Have Not Done That
Ernestine Coleman-Dupree

You know what? You could have not done that.

This may come as a shock to you, but not doing the fucked-up thing that tore so many people apart was an actual option for you. You didn't have to go through with it. You could have told me she was coming on to you. If you didn't have the balls to say no, I could have and would have gladly taken care of it… it would have been as simple as not letting her back in my house, or as complex as delivering the curb stomping she surely deserved. She was my sister after all, and you were my lover…surely there were so many other choices both of you could have made.

But neither of you did and here we all are. No one really speaks; the bridges are burned; bonds are broken. And for what? I knew what her reasoning was. Age-old sibling rivalry shit there. No surprises. But the curiosity for your reason has always been there, just under my skin, like an itch that could never be scratched. The other night, for whatever reason, that itch reached critical mass and after all this time, I decided to ask you. It's been what? Eighteen years now? I figured it wouldn't really be a big deal or hurt much to finally know why. I was wrong.

To know all this emotional turmoil, distance and discord was all due to her wanting something of mine, and you wanting to have "bang sisters" crossed off your checklist, proved to be too much.

If the smoke coming from my tears were any indication, I guess there was a little left of that bridge to burn after all.

Dysfunctional Marge
PS Warren

Marge,

I wish I could say this to your face. But you and your family are so crazy I'm terrified of what you would do.

These last ten years have been hell living with you, your weird kids, and insane parents. But I have a confession to make. I did not begin a relationship with you because I was in love with you. You were dysfunctional. Your kids were suffering, and I was asked, by mutual friends, to help. My only purpose was to make sure your kids did not turn into ax murderers, which was a real concern.

When I was confident that they would grow up reasonably sane, I left. Even though you have turned the kids against me because I married a man, I am pleased to see that all of you are doing well.

But I never told you what I thought of you. I experienced you as a backbiting, obnoxious, self-centered, self-important leech. You discounted me behind my back, to my face, and anything you gave required great sacrifice to pay back. You and your family were emotionally abusive. I lost all respect for you, and I take credit for all your successes.

As requested, I don't intend to have any further conversations with you or your kids. I wish you well.

Anna

Hello Again
Madison Diguilio

Hello Again,

It's been how many years? I'm pretty happy about where you exist in my mind. Which is that you really don't. I just find humor in the whole situation now. What I don't find humor in is that you really won't take the hint.

I can't block you; I can't delete your number; I can't actively tell you I'm not interested in being friends. It doesn't land. I'm honestly just letting you exist in your space however you'd like because that's the only way I won't receive a disingenuous apology after every few months of (much needed) silence.

Despite how this may sound, I'm not angry at you anymore. You hurt me in ways that changed me, but I've grown a lot since. You took advantage of me in more ways than one and spun it like it was my fault. And I believed you.

You have no idea how much I believed you; how many unsent apologies I wrote; how the guilt made me feel uncomfortable in my skin.

You made me keep secrets from my loved ones. You threatened me with my body in ways that I tolerated because I was young and didn't know any better. And you scared me.

You scared me so bad that I would shake while reading your texts and hearing your voice.

You told people I was an attention whore and that I never listened. I was vulnerable because I trusted you. I let you wrap me into this dangerous space where it was you and I against the world, but then you'd turn against me too.

You repeated back my insecurities like a broken record, laughing while I tried to hold myself together, and then you'd blame me. And I blamed myself too.

I was angry with you constantly but would just as constantly make excuses for you. When I was with you, the world was tense, sometimes exciting, but frightening in ways that kept me up at night. I thought that was just a part of love.

I am forgiving. I've forgiven people before you and people after you. But you used me while I was still learning to protect myself. I'm sorry, but there are some wounds time won't ever heal.

It's nice that you think so highly of me, but I won't ever forget the way you gaslit, used, and abused me. I can't. I can't be your friend because how can I ever look my inner child in the eyes and tell her I love her if I allow you a place in her future.

You're one of those people who stays stagnant no matter how much time passes. You're like a pocket dimension of my past that I've long let go of. The way you talk; the way you persist; your whole personality.

I know what you've been through, and I'm so sorry. You were a child. And I know who you are is only in place to protect your own inner child. The abused became the abuser. Your past will never be your fault, but you control who you choose to be now. We're adults.

My peace and forgiveness and compassion make my existence whole and complete. You don't need my friendship, and I'm so sorry, but I don't want yours.

You can stay or you can leave, or you can lurk, but my mind is made. I'd wish you the best, but I gave my well wishes a long time ago.

The Five Stages of Turning into You
Rebecca Grenham

To The Man Who Raped Me:

You remember me, right? We went out a few times in college. You were a senior and I was a sophomore. We met at a party. It was before dating apps became a thing.

For our first date, we tried to go to a museum. You looked bored at the bus stop, and grunted when I asked how your day was going. We got to the museum, and it was closed, so we went to a coffee shop instead. You told me about how boring you found women, and I nodded along, even though I didn't agree.

I wish I hadn't nodded as you belittled other women. I also wish I hadn't gone back to your house after coffee. I wish I had stood up right there, pushing the table back dramatically like in the movies and shouted no, I will not put up with this. But I didn't.

I wanted to please you. I wanted to not be boring, to not be like those women you hated. We talked about those other girls, the ones you despised, back at your house that night. We kept talking for a few days until I came to your house a second time later that week. I really, really wish I hadn't done that.

I wanted to be a cool girl, one that you'd be proud to date, one that you'd love tenderly. I wanted to be friendly, fun, and flirty. Instead, I ended up like you. It didn't happen immediately. It took a few stages. The five stages of turning into you.

After you did what you did, I got scared. I started scurrying to my dorm after class, even in daylight, too nervous to be in public. At night, I'd leave my bedroom light on like a child afraid of the dark. When Uber launched, I refused to take one by myself, knowing what men could do to women in dark spaces. I stopped talking to men, too, did you know that? They reminded me too much of you.

The fear then turned into rage. My body would shake while lying in bed, thinking of how much sleep I'd lost because of you. I signed up for a kickboxing class, fantasizing about punching you in the face, kneeing you in the balls, beating you bloody. I always won our imaginary fights. In real life, when I saw you that time in the library, I ran to the bathroom and cowered in the stall like an animal hiding from a predator.

Once the rage subsided, sadness set in. Instead of shaking and trembling, my body stopped moving altogether. Getting out of bed was no longer a possibility. Waking up at all was a win. On the days I did get up, I moved so slowly I could feel people get annoyed, peeved by how much space I was taking up. I was annoyed at myself too, because who else would be so silly to make a big deal out of one night in one house?

Then anxiety creeped in. Big, cascading trembles took over my body, causing me to shake uncontrollably when someone brushed into me on the street, to feel faint when I heard a rape joke, to shudder when men walked by. My friends tried to help me, but I'd stopped trusting them months before, knowing what people were capable of, thanks to you. I worried they'd take your side, that they'd say it was my fault, that what I thought had happened hadn't actually happened. Though of course my friends would never actually say that. Only you would.

After anxiety came apathy. Caring was too much effort. What was the point of it, anyway? Why even bother? People suffer from a lot worse than what you did to me. I'd tell myself the same thing every morning: "it's time to get over it." That became my new goal. Years later, I'm still not sure if I've succeeded.

You got what you wanted. Not only did you do what you did, but you also molded me after you, made me in your image. I got angry, just like you, but also scared and anxious and sad all at once. I saw what you saw. People were boring and none of it mattered. Everything was a game, and one you need to win. If you lost, you'd end up like me. Violated.

After all these years, I'm finally growing sick of being like you. I want to like people, to trust them, to care about them and their problems. I want to laugh again, really laugh—the big belly kinds that shake you at your core and crack your face into a grin. I want to sing again, to hum as I clean up, to turn the volume up on the radio and belt out the lyrics while I drive. I want to do all the things I stopped doing after I met you.

I'm slowly becoming less like you. I go to karaoke nights and shout along to the words. I cry. I laugh when someone tells a joke, even if I don't find it funny, because I respect the attempt. I'm making an effort. It's tiring, and sometimes I hate it. But anything beats being you.

Sincerely,

Rebecca Grenham, the girl you raped

CHAPTER SEVEN
LET ME EXPLAIN

"Being held accountable is an act of generosity and compassion. It is a gift that someone gives us to correct our wrongs, unlearn, and do better for the sake of our own growth. It might be uncomfortable, but it is worth the discomfort."

—Minaa B.

Holding oneself accountable for something takes a great deal of self-awareness and maturity. While we prefer to live our lives untethered, free to do and say what we please, we sometimes feel the need to explain our position, or hold ourselves accountable for events that have transpired. And while it is an almost uncomfortable thing to do, it can result in a slight sense of relief, maybe even significant dignity. How we choose to say our piece varies, from letters to phone calls to text messages or emails.

I often find it easier to express myself on paper rather than bear an awkward face-to-face interaction. It's difficult to think on my feet during a verbal confrontation. On paper, I can take my time, analyze every episode, break down a situation or thought bit by bit. Of course, that is not the case for everyone. Some folks prefer the physical nature of an in-person conversation, finding it quicker and perhaps less time-consuming. This may be true, but I find that the intimacy of the moment between the writer and the reflections that arise allows for a proper dissection of each thought, each revelation, and each word. Other times, well, it's just much less intimidating to compose a quick email while cloaked under a safe, heated blanket, or carefully and articulately write up a detailed handwritten letter, while in the safety of your own bedroom.

Yes, oftentimes, holding oneself accountable simply sucks. But we do it: because we care; because we feel guilty; because we are indeed responsible; or because it's just the "right" thing to do. The contributors below choose to share their truth on paper—it was better for them this way. Their honesty and boldness shine through the pages, and momentarily makes one wonder: how would I have handled this issue? How would I…explain?

Don't Worry About Replying
PS Warren

Dear Nelson,

I'm sure you are wondering why I'm writing you after thirty-nine years. I heard your father died a few years ago and I've pondered writing this letter ever since. Why now? Well, I'm getting older, and I need you to know the truth.

Leaving you was the most difficult thing I ever did. Yes, I know that is hard to believe given the last letter I sent you. You see, your father came to me and said he would make your life miserable if I didn't leave you. He wanted you to have a submissive wife with no other ambitions than to have your children and serve you in every way.

I tried to tell you so many times, but I couldn't come between you and your father. When we divorced and remained friends, he was not happy. He wanted you to hate me so you could get on with your life. The last letter I sent to you was worded by him, for that purpose. *"You mean nothing to me"* and *"I don't have time for you"* were his words, not mine. When you told me you would never forgive me for saying that and you never wanted to see me again, I understood. But I want you to know that I have thought about you every day since, every anniversary, every birthday, every holiday.

I'm glad to see you moved on with your life, getting married and having children. I hope your life has been rich and joyful. But most of all, I hope your father left you alone to live your life as you wanted.

I promise not to contact you again, and I won't be around much longer, so don't worry about replying.

Sue

Dear John
Amy Cotler

Dear John,

I can't live in your apartment. It's dark in there and I can feel the weight of something I don't like. The paintings on your walls strain against their hooks, longing for the floor. There's always the sound of a TV commercial in the background, even when the box is switched off. Your kitchen reeks of dirty potatoes—peeled and aging on the counter from neglect.

I'll never live in your apartment, though your kisses deeply move me. I love you for those smooth lips, that tight ass and large teeth too. But I can't step inside, more or less live, in your funky apartment, or even walk through your yard, where the grass lays flat. Even the daffodils can barely stand up to face the sun.

Sweet invitation, though. See you tonight.

— *Mary*

Love, Jaclyn
Jaclyn Roth

May 2, 2019

Dear Hannah,

It's hard for me to explain my current state because it's so murky and complex and I struggle to put into words the anxiety and frustration I feel. I want you to know that my fickle emotional state has nothing to do with you. You are my beacon of light, and you help me get through the day. Just knowing that I can come home and snuggle up next to you makes me feel better. I think a lot of my insecurities and fears about my career are manifesting themselves in other aspects of my life and I do not want them to affect you, but I know that they do. I do not want to inflict my sadness upon you. That is the last thing I want. As I reflect on my emotions, I recognize that it is a combination of factors – I have pushed my body to its limit, I am extremely overtired, and life seems very up in the air at the moment. I honestly don't know where I'll be in a couple months or a year and that kind of scares me. But life just seems so mundane – get up, go to work, do the things, and then go home and make the most of the night that lies ahead. The predictability crushes me. And then I must make the decision of working on my goals and hanging out with friends. It's a delicate balance that is not always easy to find. I'm not using this as a "woe is me" moment. I don't want sympathy or pity or concern. I don't really need anything. I just want you to know what I've been thinking about and what goes through my mind. And I know I've explained it before, but the process of writing takes me into my introverted self, and it often makes me quiet and anxious and uncertain. I guess you can say it's a catch-22. I love to write, but it brings out a version of myself that I don't always like. I'm really trying, but right now I'm struggling to be the bubbly, outgoing, fun version of myself. I know she'll be back, but it's hard for me to bring her out right now. Unfortunately, it's not something that will change overnight. It's going to be an uphill battle for me for a while. I still have a lot to figure out – and the last thing I want is to bring you down in that process. I'm on a solo journey right now and while it's mine, I would still like you to be there, but I understand that it's not easy handling my capriciousness. I've been feeling very uncertain about our relationship because I feel like I learn so much from you, but I don't know how I help you, if at all. The last thing I want is for this to be a one-sided relationship. It must be symbiotic, but I don't know if it is, and I guess I need reassurance that you do reap some sort of benefits from being my partner. I love you so much – so much that it hurts me to see me hurt you by being sad and frustrated and overwhelmed. I hope this helps you understand.

Love,

Jaclyn

Dear Friends
Jill Egland

Dear Friends,

I've been out of touch with so many of you—in some cases, for several years. Others, I've used texting as a substitute for real communication. This is a difficult letter to write. And I can't even tell you why, really. Maybe it's because Saturday was my birthday. Maybe it's something else entirely. Whatever.

So, I was at my therapist's a couple of days ago, right? And I'm doing the typical talk-weep thing, mostly around whether I should take an antidepressant of some kind. And bottom line, it boils down to this: I can't stand the thought that I might not be able to do it myself, you know? And furthermore, that there might not be an actual "it" to do. Like a diabetic needing insulin to keep things in balance, it might just be that I require some sort of serotonin-booster to keep things in check, like, forever.

But today I sit here in the Bell Tower Club waiting for my salad, and a dead chick is boxed up and laying in state in my closet. Her name is Frida. She was a week old. Yesterday I noticed she wasn't well, I picked her up and held her, tried to give her water, keep her warm. Within a half hour she was dead. I couldn't stop crying.

There was something so immense about the experience; witnessing the life leaving a creature, wishing there was some way to keep the life from leaving and not knowing how, and at the same time knowing that I wasn't supposed to, but feeling that my own humanity was somehow hinged upon trying.

My whole life is like that right now. I'm experiencing the slow draining away of my energy and life force in how I perceive myself, in my relationships. Well, it's not my whole life. Just pivotal portions of it.

I love you all. When I've finished my salad, I'll go home and bury Frida.

-Jill

A Note for My Children After I'm Gone
Karen Southall Watts

The box weighs just over four pounds, and sometimes I imagine it pulsating in "tell-tale heart" style in the bottom of the old suitcase where it lives. It's full of my journals from the months when my marriage to your father was crumbling and my mother died. I'm sure you remember those days. I had a breakdown then. I don't remember what you were told about that. Why do I know how much a pile of journals weighs? At some point in the past, I thought I might have to mail them to myself to keep them secret. I probably should have burned them.

That's an odd thing for me to say, considering I have spent a lot of time in my career telling students and budding business owners that they should take up journaling. Recording your successes, writing down your goals, journaling, or what we used to call keeping a diary, is a practice that's enjoying almost universal acceptance and praise these days. Yet, many thoughtful people I know, even those of us who recommend the practice, find it a hard discipline to maintain. During a cold and wet evening walk, a friend gave me a hint as to why.

"I only journal when I'm in agony" she said. Though I immediately countered with the prevailing, *"experts say we*

should be keeping gratitude journals," I realized it has always been the same for me.

At some point during the Covid pandemic lockdown, I pulled out my journals to look for a bit of creative inspiration. I was hoping for an idea or two that would be real, genuine, and publishable. What I found were scribbles, some barely legible, of a frightening and dark time I barely remember, though it wasn't that long ago. I had written in agony. Reading my own words years later didn't provide me the creative motivation I'd hoped for, but instead left me wondering how I'd survived.

I loved being a mom. I enjoyed life in rural North Carolina. Most of my life at that time was filled with playing, cooking, gardening, and making a cozy home. I didn't write about any of that.

My marriage lacked the grand, fairytale-esque romance I'd dreamed of since junior high. I could never find work that paid enough to cover childcare, and financial worries haunted me. Your father and I never figured out how to create the middle-class lifestyle we wanted, and the world told us we needed, with working-class wages. We fought over everything from credit card debt to wet towels on the end of the bed. Desire alone does not make one a good spouse or parent.

I started writing about my discontent. I was lonely, tired, and classically depressed. It would be years later that I realized everyone else in the house was miserable too. It's hard to see over the rim of your own cup of sadness.

A particularly frightening entry read, *"I can't remember if I fed the children today."* There were a few pages where I had been keeping a running count of the days left until you were both no longer minors, so I could disappear, or die. Many of these dark rambling thoughts were the fruit of Lorazepam, prescribed by an ever-so-helpful doctor, who saw me once.

After about two weeks, when I stopped taking medication, and started trying to live again, I stopped writing in my journals. I boxed my problems up. Sure, I continued to write over the years for business, emails by the thousands, and even some fiction and poetry, but I couldn't settle back into a daily diary habit. Perhaps it's for the best.

So, kids, if between the time I write these words and my final reckoning, I do not: find an abandoned fireplace, discover how to have a legal bonfire in town, or spend quality hours with a paper shredder, do yourselves a favor. When you find a busted old box, with a card taped to the top that reads *"4.4 pounds"* just chuck it in the trash.

Dear Patient
Jen Baker-Porazinski

Dear Patient,

I'm leaving.

We've been together for years, decades even. I've cared for you and your children. I've watched your grandchildren grow in the pictures you proudly share with me from your phone. We've laughed and cried together. It has been my great privilege to care for you, but I really must go now. Let me explain.

I've dedicated much of my life trying to be the best doctor I could be. The responsibility of caring for you, and all my patients, came at a personal cost. Like many before me, and many who will follow, I'm simply worn out. I will miss the patients I'm leaving behind. I will miss you.

I suspect you have no idea of what really goes on outside the exam room, so let me share it with you here. Like many doctors, I spend hours of time before and after the actual workday at my computer. I mindlessly eat lunch there, tapping away at my crumb-infested keyboard in a futile effort to get ahead. I do this so when you arrive, I can focus my attention on you.

What exactly do I do all this time? Mostly I work through tasks in my endless inbox - addressing phone calls, prescription refills, specialist reports, test results, insurance inquiries, hospital records, visiting nurse updates, and nursing home concerns. I fill out forms for handicap parking and write letters to employers and parole officers. I write jury excuses. These are necessary but dispiriting tasks since, despite all efforts, my inbox will inevitably fill up again. And, when the day is over, I often bring my stress home with me - worrying about my patients.

Every few nights I'm on call, and this I won't miss either. I dread waking in the dead of night to a shrill beeper alerting me that someone's in trouble. It wouldn't be so bad if, when the call was over, I put my phone down and fell back asleep. But that's not usually what happens. Minutes, even hours, tick away before my mind finds peace. I take solace knowing my help is both needed and appreciated.

There are some, though, who take advantage of this 24-hour availability and call after hours with inconveniences rather than emergencies. They call Saturday night with symptoms they've had for two weeks and Sunday morning requesting prescription refills. I try not to be aggravated. They may not realize that when I'm on weekend call, I still have to go to work on Monday.

Despite this, I hope that when you came to see me you felt like you were my only concern. I believe you deserve this respect from your doctor. I hope, though, that my focused attention doesn't make my departure seem even more personal. I'm sure you're asking: *How could I leave even you?*

I may have been able to hold out a bit longer if it weren't for the pandemic and the unbearable grief and anxiety reflected in every patient I see. I worry about the school children where I serve as medical director. I worry about the nursing home where I care for vulnerable elderly patients, lonely with isolation. I worry about sick, fearful patients not seeking help, burnt-out colleagues, and the dire shortage of mental health care in a society so deeply suffering.

I'm also less tolerant, yet another indication it's time to leave. Against my rational mind, I'm offended by patients who outright lie to my staff during Covid screening so that they can keep their routine appointment with me. Don't they realize if I'm exposed that I'll expose others? I take it personally when patients refuse vaccination, knowing the cost frontline healthcare workers are paying for their choices.

To be clear, my decision to leave has nothing to do with you. It has nothing to do with the dedicated doctors, nurses, and staff I work with, who are also struggling. Like me, they'll endure until they can't. Taking care of patients is an exhausting undertaking, especially in a country that doesn't provide everyone health care. *What good is a doctor if you can't afford to see her? How important is her knowledge if, to follow her advice, you must choose between food and medicine?*

For you, dear patient, I may have put up with my grievances for another decade if I believed that health care in America would radically change in that time. But lately, I've felt more and more helpless in this broken system. I've lost faith. I can no longer ignore my resentment toward the bureaucratic inefficiencies that steal my time or the crushing responsibilities making me unhealthy in mind, body, and spirit. The truth is my departure is overdue. I'm sure you'll be fine, but your unwavering trust in me makes leaving more difficult.

Knowing all of this may help you understand why, when offered a position at a wellness center, I just couldn't turn it down. I hope it makes a difference to you that I'm not just running away, but heading toward a holistic path that I feel passionate about that's based on partnership rather than prescriptions - one that harnesses a team of caregivers to teach valuable lifestyle skills like how to eat well, embrace physical activity, and manage stress.

Ironically, I'm leaving to give my future patients the kind of care that my intuition and vast experience have taught me people need. And, in my seemingly selfish pursuit, I'm actually modeling self-care. As painful as it may be, if the environment contributes to dis-ease, change is necessary.

I believe health is more than just the absence of disease. I dream that one day holistic care becomes standard treatment for all Americans, not just those who can afford it. I hope it will be available for you. I know you feel abandoned, but I believe our mutual respect and care for each other will help you understand why I'm leaving primary care. I believe, in time, you will forgive me.

I hope I can forgive myself too.

CHAPTER EIGHT
UNUSUAL ENCOUNTERS

*"From the beginnings of literature, poets and writers
have based their narratives on crossing borders, on
wandering, on exile, on encounters beyond the familiar.
The stranger is an archetype in epic poetry, in novels.
The tension between alienation and assimilation has
always been a basic theme."*

—Jhumpa Lahiri

What classifies as an unusual encounter? As I pondered
on a title for this section, an image of awkwardness
appeared. Discomfort followed, then bouts of uneasiness.
There is mystery in these encounters. A bit of confusion
maybe. And a pinch of wonder.

My unusual encounters have never been the same—they
vary from an extremely grateful middle-aged man randomly
striking up a conversation with me about blessings as I
waited for my Uber to arrive, to my religious driver's
education teacher dragging me to a nondenominational
church mass, where all the attendees started speaking in
tongues as I stared in bewilderment, to learning how to play
Gin rummy with an elderly patient at the psych unit. It seems

that I have so far lived quite an unusual life, filled with many rare engagements and occurrences.

Think back to your own moments of bizarre incidents, odd encounters or unique experiences. What makes them so unusual? What do you make of them?

One of the Other Six

Sarah E. Morin

Dear Doppelgänger,

I'm sorry I don't know your name. I should have asked, but I didn't know how to speak Czech. In retrospect, maybe you spoke English perfectly, but were as speechless as me to see your face on somebody else.

Even without a name, I remember you exactly, all these years later. I rose from the table to find the restroom, sidled through the bustling crowd at the restaurant, and looked into my own eyes. Had I almost run into a mirror? No, my reflection was carrying a tray of goulash and sirloin on her shoulder.

I stared at you. You stared at me. The same nose, thick eyebrows, long straight hair, tall round body. You even had three zits on your chin, too. All but the tiniest details checked out.

Even with the language barrier between us, I knew you were thinking the same thing. It was written in the shock in your own blue eyes. Had someone started cloning humans?

"Excuse me," I mumbled, because we shared no language, just a form, and because the whole experience was dissociative as hell.

When I returned to my table, my friends elbowed me. *"Did you see that waitress? She looks just like you!"* So, I hadn't imagined the resemblance. The waitstaff stole glances at me from the kitchen door. But you weren't waiting our table, and I said nothing else to you the whole meal. Now and then I caught you studying me as I studied you, like an extra jigsaw piece in a puzzle that is already completed.

I apologize if I was rude. No one trains you in etiquette for how to greet your doppelgänger. I didn't know how to ask for your name and email address. That seemed creepy, anyway. I was just another foreigner at your restaurant. Had I been more outgoing, I might have asked someone to snap a picture of us. But I didn't even know how to feel. Upset at your plagiarism? Thrilled to find the lucky lottery ticket of this once-in-a-lifetime meeting? When I was six, I pretended to be Hayley Mills at summer camp, stumbling upon my lost twin. Here I was, living out that iconic scene in *The Parent Trap*, and all I could do was try to digest the weirdness and the schnitzel. My skin itched from the flabbergasted eyes of our friends and coworkers as they dissected our every mutual feature. Were you disappointed to look like me? That was silly. You looked like you, and neither of us were less the original version than the other.

Scientists say, statistically, every person has six doppelgängers. There are whole websites dedicated to finding your twin stranger. Now and then I still read a clickbait article about it. The blond Californian skater dad who meets up with his exact replica from the East Coast, and they've both married Tiffanys and own German Shepherds. How similar were we, under our identical surfaces? I know what guided my steps to bring me to that popular hole-in-the-wall restaurant in the Czech Republic: a happy childhood in rural Indiana, college ambitions of composing Broadway shows, and a passable talent in low brass. What steps brought you to serve melt-in-your-mouth schnitzel to tourists in that castle town? Were you born and raised there? Did you play an instrument, too? Where did your path lead, after our odd encounter? I wish I knew where to direct this letter, so you could tell me.

That tour through Europe with my college band was just over two decades ago. Wow. That was another time. A time when we could breeze through airports without the ghost of 9/11 or the specter of Covid haunting us. What chance do we humans, aside from those with photographic memories, have of remembering a face they saw but once, so long ago? I have only to look in the mirror to see yours. Imagine the hair a shade darker, the head just a half-inch lower. Only, no. Even my own face has shifted in the years since. Frown lines between my eyebrows, smile lines at my mouth. I see how the stress of caregiving has left my eyes half asleep. Would we still look so alike, now?

Would I still recognize me in you? Do I still recognize me in me? That college girl who thought she would be the next Sondheim and fell in love with the history museum field instead? Who married her college crush eighteen years after he turned down their first date? Who stayed up nights pecking a novel into existence, and eventually published it? Some dreams do come true. Others don't. And we must make peace with all the divergent paths of life, for we can only walk one. I like to imagine us–you, me, and our other five doppelgängers–each living the dreams the others didn't have time or circumstances to see through.

Maybe you never thought of me again. But I have thought of you, at random times. See, I feel this odd connection to you. I hope your life has been generous. If you wanted love, or children, or to travel the world, or a successful career in bioengineering, I hope you got it. I hope you never wanted for opportunities or happiness. Perhaps our meeting and our genetics were a roll of the dice. But I like to think we were meant to cross paths. I think the world would be a better place if we all knew that scattered across the globe are six other people just like us.

Best wishes, twin stranger,

One of the Other Six

Fwd:
Dagne Forrest

I'm not sure at what point you began to send me emails with no message. Forwarding an enticing article about a place we'd shared all those years ago, the thrill of the familiar was blunted by the absence of you. You didn't even sign the body of the email, didn't even add a one-word explanation like *"This!"* or *"Remember?"* If forwarding an article to, say, a colleague, surely you'd punch in a quick *"FYI"* or *"vis-à-vis our chat yesterday"*. Surely, I deserve at least that?

The first few times it happened, I was so keen to connect, I spilled over with details from my own life, assuming you'd share the same. You never wrote back. It reached a point where I responded only to ask you never to send me an email like that again unless you also bothered to write something – just a few lines about your life in the years since we'd last seen each other. Something. Anything.

That must have been five years ago. Five years of silence. Of absence from my inbox. Until last month, when you did it again. I wonder what your drive-by emails mean, but you've given me nothing to work with. So, I hit delete. Again.

From the Other Woman
Valkyrie

Hi,

I've sat down to write this letter a thousand times and each time was overwhelmed by guilt. Not the guilt that I am betraying both your marriage and my own by sleeping with your husband, but the guilt that comes with knowing that I have no intention of stopping. Perhaps I should explain. Neither of us intended for this to happen. Both of us fought the emptiness inside that comes with having a spouse that you love with all your heart, even though they can never fill it completely. To be honest, I was desperate for you to know. Unlike the movies, there is no thrill of sneaking around for me. When I think about your reaction when you find out, my stomach knots up and I vomit. Every single time.

You and I were friends once, good friends. But as I fell deeper in love with him, I instinctively pulled away from you. I tell myself that I've done so in order to minimize the hurt for whenever you catch us, or he tells you. But so far that hasn't happened. You see, he's become my best friend. My best friend in a way that you never were. He gets me. He doesn't judge me. He understands my anxiety and my history. It doesn't bother him when I'm demanding and he doesn't care if I make dinner or not, because you will do all of that for him, I imagine. I'm the woman you can't be because you are too busy being a great mom and dutiful wife. I will never impose the same expectations on him that I do for my husband. I don't want his money or even his loyalty, only his heart.

There have been times when I pulled away from him because it felt impossible to love him this much and not have him be mine and mine alone. I got over that feeling after the first year. We belong together as much as we belong with our spouses.

We talked last night, and we were wondering if you would be open to a polyamorous relationship. That way we wouldn't have to hide. Don't get me wrong, we don't kiss in public or act a fool going to bars and clubs. We don't want to even be seen together. We would never embarrass you or my husband that way. Believe it or not, we respect the hell out of you both and neither of us want to replace either of you in our lives. It's confusing and awkward as hell to say this but we need you guys as much as we need each other. The times when we don't talk so we can stop feeling this fucking guilt is like hell for us both. It is terrible when we can't have each other, when we can't kiss away the pain and stress of the week, when we can't fuck out our frustrations.

I'm not writing this letter to cause drama in your relationship, and I would never want you to get divorced. He *needs* you. I am writing this letter to ask for your forgiveness and your permission. I don't want to be that other woman that ruined your marriage, your family or your life. I don't want to be the woman who takes from the joy of other women. I am only asking for you to share a piece of him with me. I cannot be what you are in his life, and I am satisfied with that. Still, I cannot replace what he has become in my life, and I cannot continue to live with the guilt. I am sorry that I ever let him kiss me that night; I honestly still wish it never happened. When my imagination is going wild, I sometimes wonder if you left us alone on purpose. If you knew this would happen and would condone it. It's time for me to know the answer to that question. Regardless of my betrayal or if we never speak to each other again, I just need to know if I can share him. May I please share him, with you?

-From the Other Woman

CHAPTER NINE
NOTE TO SELF

"Note to self: Never ride a motorcycle
in stilettos and a miniskirt."

—Maggie Grace

There is something so profound about a "note to self", whether it's a simple reminder to take the garbage out later, a tiny grocery list, a small affirmation, or a short diary entry.

I've probably written over a million to-do lists, a thousand diary entries, and hundreds of mantras and affirmations. They bring remembrance, safety, and comfort. I also like the concept of looking back on something I jotted down weeks, months or years ago. Notes are as surprising as letters, and I admire them for their raw, primitive, and unpolished nature. A note usually always serves its intended purpose, even if for a short moment, even if it eventually ends up crumpled in the nearby trash bin. Through every fold, every scribble and every ripple, the note remains loyal and tangible for you to revisit and simply remember.

What's the last note you wrote to yourself? Do you think it served its purpose? Did it help you remember? Did it force you to reflect? Did it serve as a cathartic release? I hope the following notes, affirmations, and entries achieved their intended purpose for their respective owners.

Dear Diary
Cindy Hossain

Dear Diary,

I write this entry again with the same shame that has accompanied many of my recent entries. It happened again last night. They are occurring more frequently; and the guilt of my sinful actions, over which I have no control, is weighing heavy on my heart.

He was in uniform as they always are - this time it was the postman. He knew how to find so much more than just a post slot. When he held me in his arms, I transformed from a human cocoon to a voluptuous woman!

I could hardly look him in the eyes this morning when he knocked on the door with parcels under his arms. Although he stood a few feet away from me, I am certain he must have felt the heat emerging from my burning cheeks. Unbeknown to him, last night we were lovers.

My darling Paul can never know of my extramarital rumpus. Throughout my pregnancy he has been understanding and has not once pressured me for intimacy. I look like a beached whale and yet he says I have never looked more beautiful. He will hint sometimes but accepts rejection after rejection without complaint. At the moment,

I cannot stand the thought of my uncomfortable body being touched - but in my dreams, I turn into a sex goddess.

I pray this will be my last embarrassing entry.

The Real Deal
Valerie Wong

i'm done with practicing love, joy and fulfillment. they say adversity's the best teacher, but i've learned enough these few years for a lifetime. i could fill wells with my wealth of experience, which feels more like poverty. some days i am utterly depleted; others i'm charged by desperate hope, even as i meander in endless circles. i am bursting with unrealized potential, raring to strike the world with bottled lightning. enough with the endless rehearsing - i'm ready to be claimed by the right opportunity.

—*the real deal*

139

From Time to Time
Savannah Moix-Rogers

An addictive personality means you overdo it, from time to time.

From time to time, I must drink all remaining coffee in the pot, so I feel worthy and deserving enough to imbibe the next day's pour.

Next day's pour quickly transitions into drinking all the water in the pitcher, so I can tamp down the caffeine overdose from yesterday and have glowing skin tomorrow.

Having glowing skin tomorrow leads to worrying that dark under-eye circles will never lighten, so I dab on lotion after lotion in hopes they will combine into a perfect cocktail.

A perfect cocktail calls, and, because there's too much vodka in the house, martinis freely flow, so I can liquidate the liquor pantry and move on to another drink.

Another drink begets another drink.

Another concern begets another concern.

But that's only from time to time.

Reflective Affirmations: On Dating
K. Cime

I'm tired of crying over men! It has been three years of riding emotional rollercoasters, and each time, I find myself stumbling off the ride a little more jaded, a little more disappointed than before.

When is it my turn? When will my love find me? I'm sick of searching for love and affection—constantly getting lost in dubious daydreams. I wonder why it's harder for me. Why I often feel that I must prove my own worth.

I'm growing weary of repetitive, petulant arguments and vexatious mind games. I refuse to shed any more tears or devote any more energy toward undeserving men who continue to make me feel less than.

From this day forward, I'll no longer entertain any bullshit!

No more broken-hearted sighs. No more painful woes. No looking back.

You'll Find Love When You Start Looking for It and Other Nonsense
Merrill Elizabeth Gray

My granddaughter smells all her food before she trusts to take a bite. I wish I would have done the sniff test before getting married. I wish that narcissists gave off a scent.

A few years ago, I was strolling down West Broadway, with my yoga mat slung over my back, and stopped inside a confectionary. As I approached the counter with my purchase, the store clerk (a man close to my age), said *"You have been with wrong man, wrong man, wrong man"* ...he repeated it many times. I laughed and said, *"Tell me something I don't know."* He's a psychic but it was likely written all over my face. He went on to tell me that I was *"like a male peacock, beautiful but easily captured."* I asked, *"You mean "naïve?"* and he asked, *"What does naïve mean?"* and I said, *"Easily captured."*

My married friends say they REALLY hope I meet someone. My 90-year-old mom says I'm not trying hard enough, and my stepdad says I'm too picky. I do admire women who are recently divorced and how hopeful they are. Most believe men will be lining up and can't wait to date, emphatic that they know someone who found love on a dating site.

I have tried dating sites over the past seven years. I corresponded with one man for a few weeks. He wouldn't disclose his last name or where he lived but he gave enough clues that my detective work found out he was married. He confessed and also told me he had Herpes 2 and took medication to keep it under control. On Tinder, someone stole my photos and used them for their profile. On Match, they've run out of suggestions for me. Mostly men make complementary comments like, *"Your photos must be really old!"* or *"I'd like to rip your shirt off."* They all want attention and if you don't give it to them in the first text, they are all *"I don't think we are a match...no questions from you hmmmm.... adios."* Thanks Narc man.

I did date one man for a few months about five years ago. He was afraid of words. I read him a love poem and he winced. I ignored it, hoping that maybe I could convince him to love me (still naïve). When he gave me bath lotion, I thought it was out of love, but he didn't like my dry skin. Critical from the start. He pouted and mopped. He consumed bottles of wine every night. In the end, after a weekend getaway, he sent me a spreadsheet with a detailed bill. He even charged me for the coffee he bought me at Tim Horton's. *Never contact me again,* I typed politely in an email.

I overhear a young girl in a clothing store *"You can only watch 'You've Got Mail' seventeen times and then it gets old."* Movies make it look effortless, but the reality is that the pilot (Andy Garcia) does not ask you for your phone number. Sorry Diane. In fact, no one talks to you on a plane.

Dating after turning 60 years old is like trying to part your hair on the opposite side. It pops back over, not comfortable with strands being manipulated. Men power walk around you, avoid eye contact, put on their mask. Dating is like walking into a room of sleeping snakes. You know many of them will bite you but can't figure out which ones.

I promise to myself that I will stop looking for love. I'll just keep reading positive memes on Instagram. *"Dating is a great way to remind you that dying alone isn't that bad."* Or *"Please stop asking me if I'm still single. I don't ask if you're still married."* Or *"Every time a man does a woman wrong God pushes his hairline by an inch."* My ex is bald.

Maybe love will find me in this city of 1.3 million people, on my quiet cul-de-sac, curled up in my cozy condo. I'll be watching Yellowstone and I'll hear the clip clop of a horse outside my second-floor balcony. And someone who looks like Kevin Costner dressed in boot cut jeans, cowboy boots and hat, will shout *"I finally found you!"* And I'll try to remember what love feels like. It's like trying to remember the exact moment you fell asleep.

CONCLUSION

Here comes the end of my small experiment turned anthology that brought plenty of catharsis to many of the contributors and submitters who responded to my call for submissions. The recurring theme throughout this anthology seems to have been reflection: reflection on the piece that was read, or reflection on your own experiences. I hope that you reflected as you flipped through these pages, and I hope that you continue to reflect as you close this book shut.

We are spread apart in location, age, beliefs and values, yet we share all the intangible components that make up our lives, like heartbreak, parenthood, grief, and so much more. We are separate, but we are bound by our unique life experiences. Those experiences sometimes mirror each other, and these are the times when we naturally come together to relate and share in those moments. Sort of like reading letters and viewing intimate portraits of strangers' lives as you recently did.

In organizing Letters I'll Never Send, I wanted to highlight daily life and the mundane parts that make up our everyday. I wanted to accentuate the random, and often stubborn thoughts that traverse our minds on a constant basis. I hope you got a taste of this effort, and perhaps even appreciated the resonance and relatability of these stories. I hope that, even if you did not connect with all the narratives shared in this anthology, that one of these stories generated a smile, a thought, or a fleeting emotion.

I hope that maybe, just maybe, you were driven to write a letter of your own. And I invite you to do just that in the last few pages of this book. Would you send it if you could?

ACKNOWLEDGEMENTS

Thank you, Wendy, for your helpful insights. Thank you to anyone who provided input and shared excitement about this project. Thank you to the contributors who made this book possible. Thank you for being open to sharing a piece of your life with the world. Also thank you for offering help and providing much-needed advice. Most important of all, thank you all for believing in me and believing in this anthology!

SPECIAL THANKS TO
THE CONTRIBUTORS

Thank you so much for your part in
helping to create this anthology!

Kayla Randolph is a poet, editor, and all-around lover of the written word. She is a freelance editor with clients including Pen & Anvil Press and Xavier Poe Kane. In 2021, she won the award of "Distinction" in the nonfiction category at the Emerson College Senior Writing Awards for the piece "Tripping Since the '50s." Her publication credits include but are not limited to *Brushfire Literature & Arts Journal, Calling the Beginning from Wingless Dreamer, Divot: A Journal of Poetry,* and the Alyssa Milano: Sorry Not Sorry podcast.

Brittany MacBeth is a creative/content writer, living in New Brunswick, Canada. She enjoys writing for all ages and has previously published spooky short stories.

Candace Cahill is a silversmith, musician, and writer living in Denali, Alaska. Her debut memoir, *Goodbye Again,* about losing her son twice, was released in November 2022. Find out more at candacecahill.com.

Angela Cheveau is a new writer with a passion for poetry and short stories. She has been published in two anthologies with pieces titled "Writing on The Wall," "Turning the Tide" and "It's Not Ok". She has also had poetry published in the *Rennie Grove Hospice* anthology, edited by Jan Moran McNeil. Cheveau has also had her words featured on the *Women on Writing* website as part of their blog and had her own story featured in *Om Yoga* magazine and *Yoga* magazine. She had her first short story published by Forget Me Not Press in 2021 and has recently had her poetry featured in the *Ey Up* anthology of Northern Poets published by Bent Key Publishing. She recently had her poem "The Foundlings" chosen for finale performance and the poem "Miraflores" selected by art installation company Stand and Stare for inclusion in the Looked After Children exhibition at the Bluecoat Chambers in Liverpool, examining the charitable origins and colonial history of the school. She hopes to one day publish her own collection of poems but until then, she is fully enjoying the journey.

Savannah Moix-Rogers (she/her) is an MFA in Creative Writing candidate at the University of Central Arkansas, where she focuses on confessional poetry and trauma poetics.

M. A. Dubbs is an award-winning Mexican American and LGBT+ writer who hails from Indiana. Dubbs writes poetry, flash fiction, and interactive/visual media. For more than a decade, her writing has been published in literary magazines and anthologies across the United States, Canada, the United Kingdom, and Australia.

French-Venezuelan **Sophie Jupillat Posey** wrote a poem about spring in the fourth grade and started a mystery series a year later. She's been hooked to creating stories ever since. She studied writing and music at Rollins College and has had numerous short stories and poetry published in literary magazines since 2014. Posey enjoys reading and writing anything from science fiction and fantasy to paranormal and mystery novels. When she isn't writing, she is composing music, creating albums, and teaching students in France. She can be reached on Twitter, Facebook, and her website. Posey is the author of *The Four Suitors* and the short story collection *The Inside Out Worlds: Visions of Strange*.

Iris Leona Marie Cross started writing short nonfiction stories in 2019. She was Gotham Writers' 25-word story winner, July 2020, and Preservation Foundation creative nonfiction contest finalist 2020 and 2021. Cross has nonfiction stories published in *The Best New True Crimes: Small Towns* (July 2020); *Storyhouse Weekly Reader* (July 1, 2020); *HELD Magazine, Issue#2 Generations* (July

2021); *The Best New True Crimes: Partners in Crime* (January 2022); *Parenthood Uncensored* (February 2022); *Resistance and Resilience Journal* (April 2022); *Dismantle Magazine,* forthcoming (Fall 2022); *LIGHT Public Health Journal*, forthcoming (January 2023). Cross lives in Trinidad and Tobago, home to a variety of birds, butterflies, and lizards. While she appreciates the beauty of the winged creatures, she has an irrational fear of those sneaky, agile, tailed reptiles that persistently try to become her housemates.

Dagne Forrest's poetry has appeared in journals in Canada, the US, Australia, and the UK. In 2021, she was one of 15 poets featured in The League of Canadian Poets' annual Poem in Your Pocket campaign. She also had a poem shortlisted for the UK's Bridport Prize and won first prize in the Hammond House Publishing International Literary Prize (Poetry). Her creative nonfiction has appeared or is forthcoming in *Lake Effect, Paper Dragon,* and *Sky Island Journal*. You can find out more about her at dagneforrest.com.

Sarah E. Morin is Premier Poet of Poetry Society of Indiana. She is a serial submitter to writing contests and has appeared in many anthologies and magazines. She has published two fairytale books: a YA novel titled *Waking Beauty*, and a children's picture book, *Rapunzel the Hairbrained*. Together with her artist friend Alys Caviness-

Gober, Morin runs the nonprofit Community, Education, Arts, whose main projects include a podcast (@theroundtable), NICE (creating art inspired by classic literature), and publishing *The Polk Street Review*, an anthology of writers and visual artists. Morin is a recently converted dog-lover and runs a youth leadership program at Conner Prairie, a history museum in Fishers, Indiana. You can visit her on Instagram - @sarahe.morin or on her websites: sarahemorin.com and cearts.org.

Valkyrie lives with her family, waiting for the world to accept that love can be ambiguous.

Abigail Hagler is a retired MD who has found a new love in writing — writing almost every day. She loves to travel and does so whenever she can manage and/or afford it. She also loves to read, daydream and learn more about the beautiful Sonoran Desert.

Brianna Malotke is a freelance writer, member of the Horror Writers Association, and avid coffee drinker. While most of her work is within the realms of body horror and nightmares, she enjoys writing love poems and drabbles. She has poetry in *The Spectre Review* and *The Nottingham Horror Collective*. Some of her most recent horror work can be found in the anthologies *Beautiful Tragedies 2, The Dire Circle, Under Her Skin, Their Ghoulish Reputation,* and *Out* *of Time.* As far as love and romance goes, Malotke has numerous pieces in the anthologies *Worlds Apart, Out of Time,* and *At First Glance* by Dark Rose Press. Along with these, you can find more of her poetry in the anthologies *Balm, Tempest, and Cherish* by Ravens Quoth Press. In fall of 2022, her debut poetry collection, *Don't Cry on Cashmere,* was published by Ravens Quoth Press. In 2023, Malotke will be a "Writer in Residence" at the Chateau d'Orquevaux in France and her first horror poetry collection will be released.

Maery Rose lives in Minnesota, where she writes creative nonfiction, short stories, and memoir while fueling herself with nature and coffee. She was awarded a Loft mentorship in Creative Nonfiction, and has been published in *101 Words, Allium, The Campus Eye* and *Minneapolis Star Tribune.*

Catherine Kenwell lives in Barrie, Ontario with her husband and four-legged kids. She is a qualified mediator and mental health advocate who writes inspirational non-fiction and short horror stories. In 2020, Catherine co-authored the best-selling *NOT CANCELED: Canadian Kindness in the Face of COVID-19.*

Merrill Elizabeth Gray's writing has appeared in Madville Publishing's *Runaway: An Anthology.*

K. Cime is a Haitian American 32-year-old woman living in Long Island. She is a registered nurse by trade, but over the years has taken up writing to express her creativity, thoughts, feelings and emotions, to alleviate depression and anxiety. This is her first published work.

Valerie Wong (AKA @theglutenfreepoet on Instagram) was born in Toronto, raised in Hong Kong and is currently a management consultant in New York. As a Third Culture Kid, she is a local and a foreigner wherever she goes. Her poetry has been published by journals around the world, including Stanford University's *Mantis*, the League of Canadian Poets' *Poetry Pause* and New Zealand's *Blackmail Press*. She is currently editing her first novel.

Cindy Hossain was born and raised in the Free State Province, South Africa. She moved to Manchester, United Kingdom in 2006 where she now raises her beautiful young family while pursuing a degree in English Literature and Creative Writing. She loves walking her dogs, reading, and writing short stories.

Kimberley Petrie is a spoken word artist and writer based in Aberdeen, Scotland. Her stage performances include Look Again festival, Aberdeen Climate Action, Extinction Rebellion Rebel Rising festival, the Doric Poetry Slam, Hysteria, Speakin Weird, Ten Feet Tall Mash Up, Like a

Blot From The Blue and Avant Garde (Glasgow). She has also appeared as 'Makar o' the Month' for the Scots Language Centre. Petrie has featured in Grampian Hospitals Art Trust 'Shop Local' exhibition at The Suttie Arts Space and in 2022 was awarded a micro-commission project from Aberdeen Art Gallery. This work was featured as part of an exhibition in the gallery and remains part of the Aberdeen Archives' gallery and museum's permanent collection. Petrie's debut poetry collection *Granite Heart* was published by Seahorse Publications in 2022.

Taisha Ostler holds an MFA in creative nonfiction from Brigham Young University. Having lived her life in the shadows of the Wasatch Mountains, her writing centers around nature, faith, and womanhood. Ostler has publications in *Dialogue, The Canticle* and *Applied Christianity*. She currently lives in Taylorsville, Utah with her husband and children.

Paula Brown is a poet and writer whose work has been published in *Anthology Nature, Tiny Seed Journal, Adirondack Review, North Dakota Quarterly, Whitefish Review,* and *South Dakota Magazine,* among others. She lives in Tucson, Arizona with her husband and a pack of dachshunds.

Brianna Little is a writer and painter born in Texas but happily transplanted to California with her amazing partner and three silly dogs. She advocates for mental health awareness on social media and is always on the journey of finding herself and her joy after trauma.

Sarena Tien is a queer Chinese American writer and feminist who is currently a PhD candidate in French Literature at Cornell University. Once upon a time, she used to be so shy that two teachers once argued whether she was a "low talker" or "no talker," but she has since learned how to scream. Her poetry and prose have appeared in publications such as *The Rumpus, Bustle, The Feminist Wire, Decoded Pride,* and *Sylvia.*

Shelley Logan lives in St. Louis with her family. Her work has appeared in *Potato Soup Journal, Little Old Lady Comedy, Moonlight Mag, Shorts Magazine,* and *FEED.* She is currently working on her first novel.

Gaby Ingram grew up in Germany. She inherited her Oma's love for traveling and exploring new places, and eventually settled in Canada. Despite her Oma's warnings, she has read many, many books. Ingram recently rediscovered her love of writing when she joined a writing circle in Parrsboro, NS. When she's not writing or reading, she can be found in her garden, or out exploring the trails and beaches of her chosen home.

Justine Manzano is the geeky author of the geeky YA series *Keys & Guardians,* and geeky YA novel *Never Say Never.* Known as a Professional-Life-Ruiner-By-Antagonist, Justine's fiction is tough on the outside and sweet on the inside, like an M&M or a hard candy with a gooey center, delivered with sass and snark. A freelance editor, she also serves as an editor-in-residence at *WriteHive*. She lives in Bronx, NY with her husband and teenage son, and can usually be found on her website, www.justinemanzano.com or all the usual social media haunts. If you've looked in all these places and can't find her, she's probably off reading fan fiction. She'll be back soon.

Emily Hockaday's first collection *Naming the Ghost* came out with Cornerstone Press in September 2022. Her second collection, *In a Body*, is forthcoming with Harbor Editions. Hockaday's work has been in anthologies and in various print and online publications. She can be found on the web at www.emilyhockaday.com and on Twitter - @E_Hockaday.

Joanell Serra is a writer and licensed therapist from Sonoma, California. Her stories and poems have been published in *Anti-Heroin Chic, Eclectica, Blue Lake Review,*

Black Fox Literary Magazine, Lime Hawk, California Quarterly, Manifest-Station and elsewhere. Her literary novel, *The Vines We Planted* (Wido, 2018), is a book club favorite. She attends the Randolph College MFA program.

Rebecca Grenham is a writer based in the U.S. Her essays and articles have appeared in various publications, and much of her work touches on themes such as mental health and surviving sexual assault. She is currently working on a novel. For updates on her work, follow her on Instagram - @rebecca_g_r.

Ernestine Coleman-Dupree has been called Tena for almost as long as she can remember. She prefers writing romance, drama and science fiction but horror, slice of life, erotica and mystery get their fair share of airtime as well. When she isn't writing, cooking, traveling or painting, she is silently taking in the world around her and the endless variety of people in it. Tena giggles more than any one person ever should and is overly fond of watching true crime shows and cheesy horror films. The unwavering support of her loved ones means the world to her, and she hands out hugs each day like most people hand out candy on Halloween. Tena has more ideas than she'll ever have time to write. Her cloud storage space is hanging on by a mere megabyte and it's a miracle her hard drive hasn't crashed due to the sheer number of words she has on file. Her love of all things written began at an early age when she didn't even realize that writing was what she was doing. Daydreams of characters living their day to day lives or off on an adventure have dominated her thoughts for decades. The first cohesive words were put on paper (more like word processor screen) in the mid 90's and the flow of ideas has yet to slow down, and she hopes it never does.

Rachel Friedman has recently embarked on a career as a freelance writer. She has published several articles, most notably in the Hack Library School magazine, *Kitchen Witch,* and the Preservation Foundation. She lives in Southern California with her family.

PS Warren has lived in many places and traveled to many more. She currently lives in Kentucky with her husband. PS Warren is the author of a novel titled *Widow's Promise,* and a children's book titled *Cabby's Garden.* Her work has also been published in the anthology, *Coming of Age Writing & Art,* by Kentucky women over 60. She has a cozy mystery scheduled for publication in early 2023.

Madison DiGuilio is a young adult who is learning how to love herself and hold her own hand through every adventure she pursues. Life can be messy, and progress isn't linear. She has accepted that she is doing the best she can, and that self-compassion is the key to growth.

Amy Cotler was a leader in the farm-to-table movement, and a food forum host for the New York Times. After her career as a food writer and cookbook author, she turned to creative writing. Her short pieces have appeared in numerous publications, including *Guesthouse and Hinterlan*d. Cotler lives in central Mexico. For more, visit: amycotler.com. For samples of her published work, visit www.amycotler.com/offerings/.

Karen Southall Watts currently writes and works in North Carolina. Her flash fiction and poetry have been featured in *Fairfield Scribes, Free Flash Fiction, The Drabble, Sledgehammer Lit, 101Words, Soren Lit, Spillwords Press*, and *The Chamber Magazine*. She is also the author of several business books and articles. When she isn't writing, Watts teaches college humanities and business courses. She received a Pushcart nomination for poetry in December of 2021. Reach her at @askkaren on Twitter.

Jen Baker-Porazinski, MD worked as a family doctor in rural New York for over two decades before joining the Health and Performance Team at Canyon Ranch this year. She has an interest in integrative, lifestyle, and narrative medicine and is writing a memoir about working in the American healthcare system, sharing both her own and her patients' stories. She occasionally blogs at https://poundofpreventionblog.wordpress.com.

Jaclyn Roth has been featured in *INK Babies, Hobart, Drunk Monkeys, Anti-Heroin Chic*, and *The Lesbian Blog*. She resides in Medford, Massachusetts with her wife and their tabby cat.

Jill Egland was born and raised in Bakersfield, California. She lived for many years in Southeast Asia, Europe, and eventually, New York's Lower East Side, all while working as a community development consultant. Egland returned to Bakersfield with her daughter and was playing in a community orchestra when she was recruited to the all-women Celtic/Klezmer band out of which, several iterations later, her current band, Banshee in the Kitchen, emerged. Today, she writes, plays accordion, walks dogs, and opines in public places.

Robbin Farr writes short forms: poetry and brief lyric nonfiction. Barely able to achieve a thousand words, her concentration on the short form keeps writing real. In addition, she is the editor of *River Heron Review*, a free-access, online poetry journal. She most enjoys the avenues of possibility that writing reveals whether she is editing the journal or her own drafts. Robbin has been published in numerous journals including *Panoply, 2River View, Atlanta Review* and upcoming in *Citron Review*. She is the author of *Become Echo* (2023) and *Transience* (2018).

About the Editor

Jackie Bluu is a writer living in Bayonne, NJ. She received a BA in Anthropology at SUNY Purchase and a Masters in Publishing at Pace University. During the week, she works full-time as a book publicist, and on weekends she manages The Writer's Den, a weekly newsletter for writers and other raw humans.

Jackie has been published in *Emotional Alchemy Magazine, Jawbreaker Zine, Thought Catalog, Awakenings, Laurels & Bells Literary Journal, Journal of Expressive Writing, Ponder Savant, Polemical Zine* and *Humankind Zine*.

Her chapbook *Facing the Beast* was published in January 2019 and *My Dear Melancholia* in May 2020. Her full-length poetry book, *(Not) Another Love Story*, was published in November 2020.

WRITE A LETTER
YOU'LL NEVER SEND: